Foreword

I feel very privileged in writing the foreword to *The Church and the Rural Poor* because it conveys a prophetic message to church people.

One accusation leveled against white Western Christianity is that it has been so engrossed in struggling for orthodoxy over the past five centuries that it has over-emphasized right teaching to the neglect of the orthopraxis. In fact, orthodoxy has been divorced from orthopraxis. As one author puts it,

> It is evident that thought is also necessary for action. But the church has for centuries devoted her attention to formulating truths and meanwhile did almost nothing to better the world. In other words, the Church focused on orthodoxy and left orthopraxis in the hands of non-members and non-believers.

And yet, St. James tells us, "What does it profit, my brethren, if a man says he has faith but has not works? Can his faith save him? If a brother or sister is ill-clad and in lack of daily food, and one of you says to them, 'Go in peace, be warmed and filled,' without giving them the things needed for the body, what does it profit?"

This book balances teaching and praxis, attempting to give a theological foundation for the action.

The Spirit of God is moving among the peoples of the Third World. There is a crescendo for self-determination and for a fair share of the material goods of the world among those who have been materially oppressed, exploited, and deprived. Theologians in the Third World, in studying the signs of the times in light of the gospels, are developing a theology of liberation expressing the aspirations of oppressed people and emphasizing the conflictual aspect of the economic, social, and political process which puts the materially oppressed at odds with those who are the oppressors.

The intensity of the conflict will be determined not by those who are materially oppressed, but by those oppressors who have an abundance of this world's goods. A complementary thrust for those in the First World would be to develop a theology of "letting go." This book is a primer in that direction being chiefly addressed to those who have.

The entire thrust of this book is very unique in that it concentrates on rural community-based economic development. After ten years of national emphasis on the urban problems, our policy makers are becoming aware that the causes of the urban problems stem from the decay and neglect of the rural areas forcing people to migrate to urban ghettos, thereby intensifying the urban situation. In my opinion, the only hope for solving the urban problem is to first reverse the rural decay and make the rural areas an attractive alternative to urban living.

Community economic development stresses community as opposed to individualism, placing "the preservation and development of the community itself high rather than low in the priority list." Its primary motivation is not for profit but for the needs of the "have nots" as they perceive those needs.

All of us must become involved, for "we all stand in need of development. Those who live comfortably need development, just as the poor need development. While in one case it is more goods which are needed, in the other it is more humanity. We all need each other in the Christian quest for community."

"The church's role in this struggle seems clear cut; we must support, in whatever way we can—politically, economically, technically—the realization of human dignity found in true cooperation—the little people's chance in a world of bigness."

From another perspective, this book is exceptional in that, with only a slight reference to ecumenism, it shows the way to true ecumenism, i.e., "working in coalition with each other." I can only re-echo and endorse the remarks of the last contributor. "You must decide what will happen in your community. Development in your community will happen only if you decide to make it happen and then act."

Rev. ALBERT J. McKNIGHT, C.S.Sp.
President, Southern Cooperative
Development Fund

Contents

Introduction

During the past several years, a movement has been taking place among the poor in rural America, particularly in the South, concerning which the church at large knows very little. It is a movement of the poor to organize in order to help themselves. In more sophisticated terms, it is called "rural community economic development." Partly it is an outgrowth of the civil rights movement, which focused attention on the plight of rural black people and which laid the base for community organization. Partly it is a result of pressures generated by the national anti-poverty programs, most of which now have been greatly curtailed or terminated. Despite opposition and adversity, the movement has continued and grown strong, providing jobs and income for a significant number of rural poor people, and bringing a new dignity and self-respect as together they determine their own future.

Within the past two years, two denominations in the South have been working together to alert their constituencies to this movement and to seek ways in which church people can fulfill a significant role in assisting its development. The United Methodist Church, through the Rural Economic Development Task Force of its Southeastern Jurisdiction, and the Presbyterian Church, U.S., through its Task Force on World Hunger, have sponsored regional workshops in several locations across the South on "Rural Poverty and Economic Development." More recently, "enablers" have been appointed in both denominations and given training in ways to relate the church and its membership to self-help efforts of the rural poor.

9

The input at the workshops and training experiences has been of such value to the participants that it was decided to seek to share a selection of these resources with a wider audience. John Knox Press kindly responded by offering to publish such resources in book form.

The materials center around three concerns: *What* are we talking about when we speak of "rural poverty" and "rural community economic development"? *Why* should the church be concerned? *How* can the church fulfill its distinctive role in relation to rural economic development?

The chapters on the "what" of rural economic development have been prepared by George H. Esser, Jr., Executive Director of the Southern Regional Council, which has pioneered in efforts to improve the situation of the southern poor; and Ben Poage, whose work with the Commission on Religion in Appalachia has led to the initiation of numerous economic development projects in rural Appalachia.

The "why" chapters have been written by professors of two southern seminaries, Methodist and Presbyterian. Both Don Shriver of the Candler School of Theology and Hal Warehime of the Louisville Presbyterian Theological Seminary are concerned with the relation of Christian ethics to contemporary social issues.

The "how" chapters relate first to the role of the church at the local and judicatory level (this chapter having been prepared by Shirley E. Greene, who has been the leading advocate for this concern among American churches), and then the wider resources upon which the church may draw as it fulfills its role (this chapter having been prepared by Norman Dewire, Executive Director of the Joint Strategy and Action Committee, through which numerous U.S. denominations plan and carry out their programs in relation to social concerns).

Particular appreciation for the Foreword goes to Father Albert McKnight, President of the Southern Cooperative Development Fund, who has been a moving spirit behind the cooperative movement among the South's rural poor.

While it is recognized that these chapters do not begin to provide a comprehensive treatment of this rapidly developing subject, it is hoped that they will help to stimulate the church to concern about the root causes of the poverty which plagues such a large segment of rural America and to response which goes beyond "putting band aids on bullet wounds" and seeks seriously to empower the poor to help themselves, in the name and spirit of him who came to "preach good news to the poor."

PART I
The "What" of Rural Economic Development

Profile of
Rural Poverty
in the South

GEORGE H. ESSER, JR.

Poverty in the South has its origins in the decision of the colonists to structure their quasi-capitalist economy around a cash-crop plantation system. The most striking feature of this system was its inability to meet the basic economic needs of any but a small white elite. Slavery and later the tenant system enabled the southern elite to maintain economic and political dominance with a minimum of opposition. The region remained industrially underdeveloped while the North developed a vast industrial base, accumulated capital reserves, and increasingly looked to the South as a source of raw materials. As a result, the region virtually became an economic satellite of the industrial Northeast. As such it developed and, to some extent, it has maintained many of the traits common to a colonial status.

In 1967 a team of economists examining the South's economy compared it with that of an underdeveloped nation. Economist James G. Maddox and three associates reported,

> ... our reading of southern history leads us to the hypothesis that the major explanation for the South's low incomes and general economic backwardness are essentially the same as those applicable to many underdeveloped national economies. That is, the South is the most underdeveloped region of the country because its social and economic structure has led to shortages of well-educated and skilled manpower, to inadequate supplies of high-quality capital, to the lack of up-to-date techniques of production, and to the paucity of innovating entrepreneurs.[1]

Since that report was published, the South has begun to

15

experience dramatic economic expansion and has undergone perhaps more changes than at any other comparable period in recent history. The region today is more urban than rural and more industrial than agricultural. Its cities—Atlanta or Charlotte or Nashville, for example—are hardly distinguishable from cities elsewhere in America except that they tend to be generally more viable. The South's population is decreasingly black (in terms of their ratio to the total population of the South) and salted heavily in its middle class with non-southerners. Culturally, the area once described as a barren desert now has the nation's first state-supported school of the arts, several nationally eminent universities, and the distinction of having produced in the twentieth century more creative literature than any other section of the country—most of it written by native southerners.

Some of the most obvious changes have occurred in the region's political orientation. Blacks now constitute perhaps the strongest single element in the Democratic Party in the South. Affluent and middle class whites have shifted their loyalties to the Republican Party in increasing numbers, although many still vote Democratic at the state and local levels. A large protest vote, rooted largely in poor and working class whites, is present and is reflected in the strong support for Governor Wallace. But more recently there has been a trend away from overt racism and toward a recognition of the importance of a concerted political effort by the poor of both races. Thus the growing use of populist rhetoric by "moderate" political leaders is matched by an awareness of the need for a coalition transcending racial divisions and having as its basis a firm commitment to economic self-interest. Signs of this development are evident in the states of the Deep South as well as the border states.

However, such fundamental changes should not obscure the fact that certain basic features of the region remain largely unaltered. Perhaps the most important of these features is that the South today retains many aspects of a colonial economy, and that a large number of its inhabitants exist in conditions normally associated with underdeveloped countries. To appreciate the reasons for this continued economic disparity and its pervasive impact on the southern people, we must take a closer look at the region's history.

Historical Perspective

The South's unique characteristics and many of its current economic development problems have resulted primarily from the plantation system and its continuing influence. The region was undergoing limited industrialization before 1840 and industrialization developed at an increasing pace from 1880 to 1900. Yet, the solidification of the plantation system—based at first on slavery and then on the sharecropping institution—caused the evolution of a number of economic characteristics that resisted the impact of this early industrialization. Long before 1900, for example, the southern states could be distinguished from the rest of the United States by such characteristics as a lower proportion of foreign-born in the population, lower levels of education, higher proportion of blacks to total population, higher proportion of agricultural to non-agricultural employment, higher fertility and infant mortality rates, higher proportion of Protestants, smaller average acreage per farm, and lower amounts of horsepower per agricultural worker. Because the plantation system dominated the economic structure of the region, few towns grew up to promote non-agricultural pursuits and to help diversify the economy. The result of these and other factors was a relatively static South at a time when the rest of the nation was developing rapidly.

The plantation system worked to the disadvantage of poor whites as well as blacks. Like the blacks, who comprised a major proportion of the population in some southern states, poor whites had few opportunities to obtain either non-agricultural training or an adequate education. They generally lacked political influence because of the elitist nature of southern politics—an elitism that manifested itself in such means of social and political control as the post Civil War poll tax.

They lacked economic power because, like those few blacks who escaped the plantation economy, they usually found only menial low-income work or scratched out a subsistance living on a small farm of their own.

The populist movement that flared briefly at the end of Reconstruction failed to deliver its promised united economic front. Conservative agricultural interests manipulated the black vote and destroyed the ability of the coalition to hang together. Consequently, by 1900, when the first great surge of manufacturing employment began to level off, a resurgent political elitism, noted for its racism, had become firmly entrenched. The poor white worker gave his support to disfranchisement for the black southerner, and political exclusion of blacks was effectively written into the law. Discrimination and segregation remained institutionalized throughout the first half of the twentieth century.

Not until the 1950's, which brought concurrently another period of rapid industrial growth and the emergence of the Civil Rights Movement, did racial segregation begin to erode and then to crumble dramatically as change generated demands for additional change. Increasingly large numbers of white southerners began to realize that the traditional social and economic system, based on segregation, was incompatible with an emerging industrial society. Not only did industrialization weaken the influence of agricultural interests but also, in a sense, it set the stage for reaction to black discontent which exerted increasing social, economic, and political pressures on the white ruling class.

Industrialization brought into the region merchants and technicians with a different political and social outlook. It brought the emergence of a trade union movement and created a demand for better education and job training. Perhaps most important, the industrial system required performance on the basis of skill instead of race, caste, or family connections.

The South Today

Despite the changes that have been wrought within the past two decades, the South today retains many of the problems—social as well as economic—that have been its lot for a century or better. Although it has lost some of its homogeneity, the region remains largely Anglo-Saxon and Protestant. It has one-third of the nation's population and still roughly fifty percent of the nation's blacks. Most significantly, the South is the home of almost half of all the nation's poor according to recent U.S. census statistics.

Continued industrialization and migration patterns, which are expected to prevail for at least another decade, will bring about additional demographic changes. However, these changes most likely will create as many problems as they solve. The population is growing slowly less native and less black, less agricultural, and altogether less homogeneous. While these changes include an increased urban population (currently 65 percent), the major shifts have taken place in and from the rural areas. The agricultural population is declining, but the total rural population is not declining in absolute numbers. Rather, it is transforming itself from rural farm to rural non-farm. A significant portion of the population have become commuters and so-called "sundown farmers," individuals who continue living on the land while commuting to a newly acquired job in a nearby city or small town and sometimes farming a small piece of land after work as an income supplement. The South is also populated heavily with former tenant farmers who neither have steady jobs nor produce cash crops in quantities sufficient to provide more than subsistence incomes.

Migration out of the region, which accounts for one-third of all migration, continues to skim the cream off the region's black population, the young high school and college graduates, mostly from the rural areas. Like ships passing in the night, they are matched by white, middle-class non-southerners moving mainly into the suburbs and working in the cities as managers, technicians, and salesmen for new industries. As those blacks with more potential move out and middle-class whites move in, a larger widening of the income gap between the races results. The rural economy is further depressed by short-range migration (within the region), with a resulting decrease in the number of small farmers and black ownership of land, and a corresponding increase in large-scale commercial farming. Black migration into urban areas from rural ones, coupled with suburban flight by whites, will foster continued increases in the black inner-city population.

Income Distribution

Unquestionably the South has achieved tremendous economic progress within the past two decades. Most statistical indicators are beginning to move towards the national averages. The problem, of course, is that the benefits of this progress have been distributed unevenly—for an even higher concentration of wealth exists in the South than in other areas of the nation. The top one-fifth of southern families in terms of aggregate income receives 43.3 percent of all income compared to 41.6 percent for the top one-fifth of all U. S. families. The bottom one-fifth of the South's families receives only 5.0 percent of all income compared to 5.5 percent for the U. S. bottom fifth. The South not only has a more unequal income distribution than the nation as a whole, but also has greater inequality of income between the races. The ratio of black to white median income for the South in 1971 was 56 percent and for the North and West together was 69 percent.

The relative position of blacks compared to whites improved substantially over the decade of the sixties in the nation and especially in the South, but this upward trend has leveled off and now actually appears to be on the decline. The ratio of black to white income rose in the nation from 51 percent in 1959 to 61 percent in 1969 and stabilized until 1972 when it declined to 59 percent. The South, relatively further behind, gained perceptibly so that it was closer to other region's ratios, but now that of the South has also begun to decline.

Despite its advancements, and partly because the benefits of progress are spread unevenly, the South today remains the most underdeveloped section of the nation; as heretofore noted, it is still comparable in many ways to a colonial economy. It has an abundance of land and natural resources. But its human resources, the most important for the region's future, are less well-educated and trained, less fully employed and adequately paid, and less prepared to function effectively in the diversified industrial-technological society that the region must develop to achieve economic parity with the rest of the nation. That is why, more than three decades after the South was described as "the Nation's Number One Economic Problem," it remains not only that but also the source of many of the nation's urban ills—in the North as well as in the South. This was made abundantly clear by the President's National Advisory Commission on Rural Poverty, which warned in its report of May, 1968: ". . . if Southern poverty leads to under-investment in human capital, the consequences may well be felt to a greater extent in the more industrialized North than in the rural South."

The commission found a causal chain between rural southern poverty and northern ghetto problems and pointed out that the causal relationship applies not only to the southern blacks but also to southern white out-migrants. The commission concluded: "The continued existence of a hard-pressed Southern rural population implies serious problems for metropolitan areas, the natural destination of rural America's surplus population." That the region's population—non-rural as well as rural—will remain hard-pressed for many years to come seems certain.

Economically, the South is still poor and improving so slowly that a majority of the next generation of southerners will not catch up to the national norm if the present rate of development continues; none of the present generation of the poor will ever catch up. Despite impressive industrial development since World War II, the region's debased wage scale and its unequal tax structure have fostered an economy that is seriously out of balance. The tax base is small, and public funds are raised through generally regressive tax policies. In all of the southern states the number one source of tax revenue is the general and selective sales tax, considered the most regressive of all taxes. In eleven southern cities in 1972, families who live on less than $2,000 a year relinquished 12.3 percent of their income in sales, excise, income, and property taxes. Those with incomes over $10,000 paid only 5.6 percent of their income in these taxes.[1]

The region's dominant manufacturing employment is in labor-intensive, low-paying industries that exploit unskilled or semi-skilled workers. Although the South is improving relative to the rest of the nation in that its labor-intensive industry is growing more slowly than formerly, the importance of this kind of industry is still greater in the South than in the nation as a whole since it comprises a larger percentage of the southern industrial base.

The Poor

Private studies have shown that the South has a larger share of poverty (44 percent of all U. S. poor persons in 1971), a larger dependent population (those under 15 and over 65), and a higher fertility rate than the rest of the nation. Southerners—black and white—are poorer than their fellow Americans anywhere else in the country, and the half of the nation's black population that still lives in the South is, of course, the poorest of the poor. The average amount needed to bring the income of black families below poverty up to the minimum poverty level in 1969 was $1,853. For southern whites in poverty, the average deficit was $1,402.

The Brookings Institution reported that in the South in 1966 44 percent of all whites and 63 percent of all blacks lived in substandard housing. Although more recent studies are unavailable, there is little reason to believe that the overall situation has much improved. The specific plight of the poor cannot be described adequately in figures. Housing might be a three-bedroom shack that rents for $15 a month and lacks indoor plumbing. Electricity frequently means a single light bulb hanging from the ceiling of each room, with a two-burner hot plate for cooking. For the very poor, it makes little difference whether the housing is located in an urban or rural setting.

Health care too often means the services of a midwife at birth and an undertaker at death. For the black male in Georgia it means a life-span eight to ten years shorter than the national average. For the black baby in Mississippi it means the highest infant mortality rate in the nation (39.7 deaths per 1,000 live births in 1970). For black and white alike it means decreased employability.

More importantly, hunger—constant and gnawing hunger —stalks the homes of these black and white southerners. Dr. Raymond M. Wheeler of Charlotte, North Carolina, President of the Southern Regional Council and member of a medical team that investigated health conditions in the Deep South, described this vividly in testimony presented in July of 1970 to the Senate Subcommittee on Migratory Labor. He stated,

> We stopped and examined children at random and almost every child had some preventable physical defect. We saw tiny youngsters drinking rice water out of bottles because their mothers had no milk to give them. Chronic skin infections, both fungal and bacterial, were practically a "normal" finding. . . . Rickets is supposed to be a rather rare disease these days but we saw one child after another with deformed ribs and legs, thickened wrists which are the classical landmarks of disease . . . and children die. Even worse, most of them live, numbed by hunger and sickness, motivated only by an instinct for survival. . . .

Dr. Wheeler's description is not of migrant children alone, but also of children who live in a community year-round— children whose continuing plight cannot be laid to the unique problems of transient labor.

As part of an unorganized, low-skilled labor force, the parents of such children most likely work in agriculture as day laborers or in a low-paying industry—probably textiles, furniture, tobacco, paper, or the lower levels of the service industry. Their average wage scale is well below that of the nation as a whole. Even if they belong to the minority of the labor force claiming union membership, it is likely the union is weak. The chances are one in three that the job they have now is in an industry that is declining or, at best, growing slowly. Poor blacks are frustrated first in their attempt to enter the economic system and again when they do gain entry. When manufacturing jobs do open up, blacks usually go to work at minimum wages with little chance of advancement, and almost certainly in a manual or low-skill service job.

Predictably, the percentage of teachers and social, welfare, and recreation workers who are non-white is higher than in other categories of professional employment. But black penetration into the professions is shallow, to say the least, and, for teachers, now on the decline. Among the South's lawyers, fewer than one percent are black. Of its physicians, slightly more than two percent are black and concentrated mostly in the urban areas. Three-fourths of the one hundred black physicians in Georgia, for example, practice in the city of Atlanta. There are no black city managers, and not more than a handful of black architects, engineers, and planners. The situation does not promise a great deal of improvement. Blacks' opportunities in public education—the single profession in the South into which they once could enter with relative ease, rise in salary and status, exert influence over direction of their work, and use their ideas creatively—have been decimated. In one year alone (1970), according to the Race Relations Information Center of Nashville, Tennessee, about one-third of Alabama's 10,500 black school teachers were dismissed, demoted, or pressured into resigning.

It is obvious that black southerners have not received a proportionate benefit from the region's recent advances. Today few either own, manage, or have access to even a minimum amount of capital. Mainly by their own efforts they have broken the shackles of segregation, but even where the law accepts them they must fight to have the law enforced. In their contact with whites they often still encounter paternalism and insensitivity. And few poor southern whites are better off except that they have a slightly better education and the advantage that accompanies their skin pigmentation.

Thus, we may conclude that despite far-reaching changes wrought within southern society and upon its institutions within the past two decades, the remnants of historic institutional practices continue to exert a strong influence upon the region.

Hence, the dilemma facing the people of the South is enormous. To build a better society, the human resources of the region must be developed. At the same time the South must expand its economy and open up its political, educational, and social institutions in order that all of its people can have access to and benefit from a productive share of that society. Clearly a greater degree of industrialization must be achieved. However, at the same time we all must realize that industrialization per se is no guaranteed panacea that will automatically cure the region's social and economic ills. Some of the nation's worst poverty exists in the midst of the most heavily industrialized cities of the Northeast.

Poverty in the South, as in the nation as a whole, must be attacked at its roots. The trickle-down theory of economic development will not solve the problem of economic disparity. Neither will political rhetoric nor piece-meal social welfare programs. Nothing less than a program resulting in redistribution of the region's wealth will eliminate the gross economic disparities that currently exist in the South. However, before a more equitable distribution of wealth can take place, it will be necessary to eradicate the last vestiges of the region's colonial status. Only then will the people of the South have control over the resources and capital that they own and produce. Only then will they be in a position to get on with the important task of creating a society characterized by economic and political justice.

The Cooperative Movement Among the Southern Rural Poor

BENNETT D. POAGE

From the broken ridges of Appalachia to the flat brown fields of Louisiana, men and women of the soil are reaching out—with their hands, their minds, their spirits—toward the hope of full human dignity for all people.

Human dignity means many things. In a religious sense, it means that every human being is of equal worth in the eyes of God.

From an economic viewpoint, human dignity means that no one shall be exploited by any other person, corporation, or government; instead, there shall be decent opportunity for every family to gain what it needs by its productive labor.

> ... the economic, while not the highest in terms of dignity, is basic to all other human aspirations, physical, social, cultural and even spiritual. For economics, or purchasing power, directly influences the realization of the other human aspirations, especially spiritual.[1]

From a social point of view, human dignity requires the end of all discrimination based on race, class, or economic condition, and the beginnings, at least, of a true brotherhood of all people everywhere. But human dignity does not come easily.

Yet, we must begin somewhere, and the logical place to begin is where the people are now—weak and defenseless with little voice to speak effectively for themselves, owning little or nothing.

> Had me a farm sitting pretty on the hill. But, if you look, you'll see it ain't there still.
> —The Pigeon Song "America"[2]

27

Alone and acting individually, the people are not only helpless, but also hopeless, which is worst of all.

But united—then they can be strong. This is why cooperatives—joint ownership of the economic and social tools that can fashion human dignity—are so important. Cooperatives are the little people's chance in a world of bigness.[3]

> For the rural poor who have few skills, no capital and little organizational experience, the cooperative approach to rural development offers a foundation of hope.[4]

Rural Development and Cooperatives

What Are Co-ops?

Today, many different enterprises are organized in a cooperative way: food, furniture, optical and drug stores, farming, handcraft production, housing, market research, and domestic services.

The word *cooperative* does not, by itself, denote a distinct type of legal entity. A useful general definition, one which includes the few factors which all of the above operations have in common, is as follows:

A cooperative is a group of people faced with a common need who meet that need by organizing to own, control, and patronize their own enterprize. The members organize their own enterprize in order to serve those who use it—not to make money for investors. They want to do something for themselves that no one else has been willing or able to do.[5]

CO-OPS COMPARED WITH CORPORATIONS

COOPERATIVE:	CORPORATION:
Nature: Organized people	Nature: Organized capital
Purpose: To serve its members at cost	Purpose: To serve public for profit
Methods: 1. Each member has one and only one vote. Democracy: the people rule.	Methods: 1. Each share of stock has one vote. Plutocracy: money in control of the few, rules.

2. Capital is paid minimum interest. Money is the servant.
3. Surplus savings are paid to members in proportion to patronage. People receive the benefits.

Results: Wealth equitably distributed among the many.

HUMAN RIGHTS

2. Capital receives all the profits. Money is the master.
3. Profits are paid to stockholders in proportion to their holdings. Money receives the benefits.

Results: Wealth centered in possession of the few.

PROPERTY RIGHTS[6]

How Co-ops Develop Rural America

Cooperatives have been very important instruments for rural development throughout the world for the past half-century. The rate of growth of rural co-ops internationally has been especially rapid during the past twenty years.

Co-ops have been most influential in rural America. Service co-ops have provided electricity and telephones to more rural families than all the private utility corporations put together. Farm supply co-ops, by providing fertilizer, seeds, and feed at volume buying prices, and farm marketing co-ops, by selling grain, fiber, and slaughter animals at pooled seller prices, have contributed significantly to the world renowned efficiency of American agriculture.

The successes of low income or limited resource cooperatives in the 1960's and early 1970's have been no less dramatic. Abt Associates, in a study of low income rural cooperatives, has listed six important benefits which low income cooperatives (LICs) have provided poor rural communities:

- Improving members' economic status (increased income and related benefits);
- Improving members' skills and abilities (especially production skills, but also general education and interpersonal skills);
- Improving the membership group's role or status in the community (e.g., by increasing member participation in community affairs);
- Improving non-production services (either through direct provision of services or by referral to existing sources);
- Improving economic conditions of the overall community;
- Reducing outmigration from the community.[7]

LICs and Economic Objectives

Most LIC practitioners believe that poverty is essentially an economic problem, that it must be attacked with economic weapons, and that these weapons must be in the hands of those who are abused and exploited by the "larger" economic system. In pure economic terms, the root cause of poverty is the people's" (those in poverty) lack of control over the flow of goods and services.

How well LICs are achieving economic objectives can be measured by looking at past cooperative growth in members' net income profits after costs of production are paid. According to government statistics,[8] per capita income in rural areas has grown 5.7% annually for the past twenty years. Therefore, assuming a median period of co-op membership as two years, a "successful" LIC should provide its members a two-year income gain of more than 11.5%. When this measure was applied to two recent studies (first, an analysis of emerging cooperatives by USDA covering a sample of 28 machinery and 20 marketing co-ops, published in 1972, and second, a study of 18 rural co-ops by Abt Associates, published in 1973), the following was discovered:

1. The USDA study, sampling 100 members, showed a net income increase of 9.5% annually, or 19% for the two-year period (7.5% above the 11.5% average).[9]
2. The Abt study, interviewing all the members in its co-op sample, showed a net income increase of 10.0% annually, or 20.0% for the two-year period (8.5% above the 11.5% average).[10]

Moreover, it must be kept in mind that the economic success verified by these two independent studies was achieved among the hard-core rural poor.

LICs and Social Objectives

Socially, cooperatives do allow individuals to express their natural tendency to join a group in order to accomplish goals not attainable individually, and yet be able to participate in plans and decisions expressed or adopted by the group. However, many LIC practitioners believe low income co-ops should go beyond such general social objectives and have or develop specific social goals. Father A. J. McKnight, Director of the Southern Cooperative Development Program, for example, states that the major problem in the rural South is as much a human (social) one as it is economic. He feels the southern rural poor are an undeveloped people, a part of the Third World who have been systematically oppressed and excluded from the affairs of the community. He further states: "In our work with cooperatives, we have found that through participation in the affairs of the co-op, people develop a sense of belonging, and that by identifying themselves with the co-op, they gradually overcome this image of self-hatred (lack of identity). Through our limited experience, we have become convinced that cooperatives are excellent instruments or tools for coming to grip with self-hatred, massive apathy and lack of social cohesion which are so prevalent among an undeveloped people."[11]

The Abt study discovered, however, that not all LICs pursue such hard social goals, but that they are added, in addition to economic goals and functions, in response to local needs or situations. The study further showed that co-ops which have strong social goals do develop a higher level of member support. However, resources are diverted in the process, thereby causing poor financial performance. Nevertheless, most co-ops which adopt explicit social goals are attempting to function with a very poor clientele and/or work in areas where the community attitude toward the co-op and its members is most negative.[12] The co-op, being responsive to its members' needs, does what it is asked to do; in these cases, it often does so in spite of a poor balance sheet.

On the other hand, established American farm co-ops are primarily economic organizations (almost never adding social goals). They rely on "supply management" in order to control markets and protect farm incomes. Consequently, they have a very dim view of combining economic and social objectives. This is because the meeting of social goals (as shown in the Abt study) might weaken the co-op economically. Here we encounter a paradox. For example, poor farmers are not welcomed as members of these established co-ops, not so much because of their economic weakness, but because of their great social need.

Ray Marshall and Lamond Godwin, in writing *Cooperatives and Rural Poverty in the South*, recognized this paradox, a problem which affects both the established co-ops as they make the hard economic decision and thereby exclude many of the poor from their ranks, and the low income co-ops as they strive to balance economic and social goals. Marshall and Godwin state that, "Although a co-op (LIC) often has social and political objectives, these objectives cannot be achieved unless the co-op is an economic success."[13]

Another author, speaking of the Appalachian experience, says, "... groups (LICs) are rarely funded to handle social aspects (goals) which are costly, so they have to be sound enough economically to afford the 'slack' necessary for maintaining the social parts."[14]

It seems reasonable to believe, based on both survey and experience, that co-ops cannot hope to be successful "economically" if they utilize all their resources for social objectives, no matter how badly social improvements are needed. Co-ops can be neither welfare nor community action (service-type) organizations. This doesn't mean, however, that LICs can't or shouldn't strive to meet certain fundamental long-range social goals which must be dealt with if the cycle of poverty is to be broken. The Abt study and the experience of LIC practitioners suggests that co-ops can be very effective in the social goal area of improving the membership's group role in community.[15]

Furthermore, "among the co-ops pursuing the group role goals, there is evidence that social and economic goals benefit each other."[16]

The cooperative's organizational structure provides for equal and democratic control of management and risk-taking, thereby, ideally, training through involvement the poor members in group planning to meet their own stated needs. Also, membership and board meetings, when properly conducted, demonstrate the advantages of free and open discussion, thereby training for personal (human) development.

LICs and Political Objectives

The use of the co-op as a special interest bloc of voting citizens to influence political attitudes and decisions at all levels of government is a reality for both the established and low income cooperative.

However, LICs have much more explicit political objectives, whether they are stated as goals or not. The very act of organizing for economic independence from the "establishment" and of providing self-help "jobs" for their poor members makes the LIC "radically" political in most southern communities. Throughout the South, one of the primary means of maintaining political power is through the control of jobs. Jobs are a scarce and hence important resource in most rural southern communities. Votes depend on who gives a job to whom. Therefore, the more jobs a man controls, the more likelihood he has of maintaining his office or position or power in the community. This conflicts directly with LICs where people are trying to establish their own business, with the jobs under their own control.[17]

As McKnight observes, "People who control the financial processes of a region, control the power structure (economic, social and political) of that region. When the poor acquire economic motivation, they also acquire a greater team spirit and responsibility in all areas of community life."[18] Further, Marshall and Godwin state, ". . . as experiences in other countries illustrate, co-ops can be used to develop political leadership."[19] Moreover, by providing greater economic independence, co-ops could make their members less vulnerable to the use of economic pressures against them for political purposes.[20]

The political objectives of LICs, then, can be stated in two broad categories: first, *explicit* political objectives, such as (a) lobbying with national and state government officials for new legislation complementary to the goals of the LIC and/or the poverty community, or with church and foundation officials for new complementary funding policies; or (b) applying political pressure for the equitable implementation and favorable interpretation of existing laws or policies which would be complementary to the goals of the LIC and the community it serves. Second, *implicit* political objectives, through the creation of local jobs and businesses, not under the control of the power structure, which, thereby, creates a local political power base of the low income members (workers/owners).

Low Income Co-ops: A History of the 1960's In the Deep South

The current cooperative (LIC) movement in the Deep South was born out of the civil rights movement of the late 1950's and early 1960's as one solution to the need of developing businesses and jobs owned and controlled by the poor.

Organizations contributing to the organizing efforts of the 1960's include: the Student Non-Violent Coordinating Committee (SNCC), the Southern Christian Leadership Conference (SCLC), and the Congress of Racial Equality (CORE) Also, a number of Catholic and Protestant church leaders were active in the promotion of LICs during this time. For example, Rev. Francis X. Walter, Director of the Selma Inter-Religious Project (Episcopal), was instrumental in founding the Martin Luther King (Freedom) Quilting Bee at Gee's Bend, Alabama. Rev. Walter also actively supported the Southwest Alabama Farmers Cooperative Association (SWAFCA). Father Albert J. McKnight, a black Catholic priest in the rural Louisiana community of Lafayette, formed the Southern Consumers Education Foundation (SCEF) and the Southern Consumers Cooperative early in the 1960's. McKnight utilized the philosophy of the Antigonish Movement in Nova Scotia in developing these organizations. McKnight was also instrumental in the development of the Southern Cooperative Development Program in the middle 1960's, out of which grew the Federation of Southern Cooperatives (FSC). Finally, by the end of the decade, McKnight's leadership had sparked the formation of the Southern Cooperative Development Fund (SCDF). SCDF was organized for the express purpose of making loans to low income cooperatives.

In addition, the Delta Ministry, an effort supported by the National Council of Churches, established "Freedom City," a 400-acre cooperative community for evicted farm workers which also gave assistance to other LICs in Mississippi. Other "church" assistance in the form of limited financial aid came from the Methodist, Episcopal, and the Presbyterian (both US and USA) churches.

In 1967, the Federation of Southern Cooperatives was formed. It provides direct grants and organizing, training, and technical assistance to its member cooperatives, which numbered nearly 100 by the end of the decade. These cooperatives affected the lives of over 20,000 predominantly black poor families. The table below shows the geographic distribution of FSC co-ops and co-op membership by type.

Other organizations, agencies, and foundations which played an important role in the establishment of Deep South co-ops during the 1960's include: *organizations*—the National Sharecroppers Fund (NSF), the Southern Regional Council, the Cooperative League of the U.S.A., the Credit Unions National Association (CUNA); *agencies*—the Office of Economic Opportunity (OEO was the main source of financial assistance to LICs during the 1960's), Farmers Home Administration and Farmers Cooperative Service (both FHA and FCS being major agencies of the U.S. Department of Agriculture); *foundations*—the Ford Foundation (the major source of private support for Deep South LICs during the 1960's), the Field Foundation, the New York Foundation, the Aaron Norman Foundation, and the Cooperative Assistance Fund (formed by a consortium of smaller foundations).

LOW INCOME COOPERATIVES AFFILIATED WITH THE FEDERATION OF SOUTHERN COOPERATIVES, AUGUST 1969[21]

Location	Agricultural Marketing and Supply		Credit Unions		Handicrafts and Small Industry		Consumers		Fishing		Others		Total	
	Coops	Members	Coops	Members	Coops	Members	Coops	Members	Coops	Members	Coops	Members	Coops	Members
Alabama	2	1,825	6	2,784	2	108	3	230	—	—	2	2,451	14	7,379*
Arkansas	1	300	1	150	—	—	2	80	—	—	—	—	4	530
Florida	4	384	1	101	—	—	—	—	1	92	—	—	6	577
Georgia	2	400	1	190	1	55	3	490	—	—	—	—	9	1,325
**Kentucky	1	10	—	—	2	55	—	—	—	—	—	—	3	65
Louisiana	3	290	4	1,833	—	—	—	—	—	—	1	2,050	8	4,173
Mississippi	5	1,875	1	500+	4	960	3	1,080	1	25	3	497	17	4,937
Missouri	1	200	—	—	1	46	—	—	—	—	—	—	2	325
**North Carolina	1	175	—	—	1	25	—	—	—	—	1	80	2	200
South Carolina	3	224	2	400	1	35	2	1,300	1	10	—	—	8	714
Tennessee	—	—	—	—	1	150	1	200	—	—	1	80	3	235
Texas	—	—	—	—	—	—	—	—	—	—	—	—	2	300
Virginia	1	300	—	—	—	—	—	—	—	—	—	—	1	300
**West Virginia	—	—	—	—	1	30	—	—	—	—	—	—	1	30
Total	24	5,982	16	5,918	14	1,474	15	3,080	3	127	8	2,702	80	2,702

* Membership totals are slightly inflated because some members belong to more than one co-op.
** LIC's in Appalachia (added by the author).
Source: Federation of Southern Cooperatives, Epps, Alabama.

In Appalachia

The Appalachian LIC development effort was assisted, during the 1960's, by the community organizing thrust of VISTA (now part of ACTION) and the Appalachian Volunteers (both organizations being a part of the young OEO's War on Poverty). These organizing efforts

> found form through informal production and marketing groups (largely handcraft) called "co-operatives." Many of these largely OEO created and funded groups failed.... By 1969, surviving groups began to gain maturity and organizational clarity. Many incorporated as co-ops or non-profit corporations. By 1970, many of these groups were striving to form larger area organizations to provide federated services.[22-23]

By late 1968, following the lead of Deep South clergymen, organized denominations began to become involved in the Appalachian LIC movement. This interest was primarily focused through the Commission on Religion in Appalachia (CORA), a regional coalition of seventeen denominations. Rev. Max E. Glenn, Executive Director of CORA, this author (now Executive Director of the Human/Economic Appalachian Development Corporation), and Monsignor Edward O'Rourke (then Director of the National Catholic Rural Life Conference and Chairman of CORA's Self-Help Task Force) conducted numerous training sessions on cooperative development throughout Appalachia. By 1969, this interest had focused in the regional development of the Human/Economic Appalachia Development (HEAD) Project and the local organization of the Grass Roots Economic Development Corporation (GREDC) at Jackson, Kentucky. By 1970, GREDC had directly sponsored two successful LICs (a feeder pig and rabbit production cooperative) and assisted in the development of a sister handcraft cooperative (OEO-funded), the Grass Roots Craftsmen of the Appalachian Mountains, also in Jackson, Kentucky.

Other significant involvement of the church during the 1960's in the Appalachian LIC movement included the United Methodist Church's Henderson Settlement at Frakes, Kentucky. Henderson Settlement, under the leadership of Rev. Robert Fulton and Jerry Mark, led Appalachian participation in the Federation of Southern Cooperatives and developed the Frakes Feeder Pig Cooperative and the Laurel Forks Craft Cooperative. The Federation of Communities in Service (FOCIS), a lay order of the Catholic church, also began to promote community economic development during the late 1960's, including a workers' cooperative restaurant, The Bread and Chicken House in Big Stone Gap, Virginia.

By the end of the 1960's, almost one hundred formal and informal LICs existed in Appalachia with thousands of low income families involved.

Other organizations, agencies, and foundations which played an important role in the establishment of Appalachian co-ops during the 1960's include: *organizations*—the Council of the Southern Mountains, the Cooperative League of the U.S.A., the Credit Unions National Association (CUNA); *agencies*— the Office of Economic Opportunity (OEO was the main source of financial assistance to LICs during the 1960's in Appalachia, especially for credit unions in West Virginia, vegetable cooperatives in Virginia, Kentucky, and North Carolina and universally for handcraft cooperatives),[24] Farmers Home Administration, U.S.D.A. (FHA was somewhat more active and successful in Appalachian cooperative development during the 1960's, making important capital loans to a number of currently "successful" cooperatives),[25] and Farmer Cooperative Service, U.S.D.A. (serving as an invaluable training and technical assistance resource for Appalachian cooperative development);[26] *foundations*—the New York and Rockefeller Foundations have been the primary and almost singular supporting foundations for a limited number of Appalachian cooperatives (primarily those relating to CORA).

Southern Cooperativism in the 1970's

Since the close of the last decade, community economic development (CED), of which LICs are one important part, in both Appalachia and the Deep South, has gone through a period of jelling. In one sense, it has been a time of tightening of budgets and objectives as the relatively free access to most "poverty" funds has dried up. It has also been a time of evaluation, both by funding sources and by the people's groups who were utilizing the various institutional tools to achieve their goals. Finally, CED has experienced growth in those settings where maturity and experience and most economic, political, and social criteria were favorable; and it has experienced erosion in those situations where institutional mismatching, imbalances, lack of maturity and/or the unavailability of necessary resources have created unfavorable circumstances.

Community Development Corporations and Local Economic Development Corporations

The idea in poverty circles in the early and mid-1960's that co-ops were some sort of panacea—that they could be utilized to cure any social or economic ill—was put to bed, fortunately for the LIC movement, by the end of the decade. In its place, a new interest sprang up nationally in community development corporations (CDCs) as umbrella organizations which could perform broader and more integrative functions than pure co-ops. CDCs were not designed to displace LICs, but to supplement and widen the local means to reach community needs which LICs had heretofore been unable to deal with, such as community planning,[27] health care, housing, and the development of more traditional profit-making industries. Many CDCs, in fact, started or related to LICs as a part of their umbrella function.[28] OEO, under its new Title VII (old 1-D Special Impact) has been the prime government funding agent of CDCs,[29] and the Ford Foundation has offered the major foundation support.[30]

A local economic development corporation (LEDC),[31] also called local development corporation/company (LDC), is an organization whose primary purpose is to foster the economic development of a specified group and/or community. There is very little practical difference, organizationally, between CDCs primarily designed for economic development and LEDCs.[32] In large part, the growth of CDCs and LEDCs has been a blessing to LICs by allowing these cooperatives to concentrate in the specific marketing, training, and technical chores they are best able to accomplish and, conversely, relieving them, by and large, of production and social service functions which they have the greatest difficulty in successfully accomplishing.

By 1973, more than two dozen rural CDCs and LEDCs relating to low income communities or groups were operational in Appalachia and the Deep South.[33]

OEO and OMBE

With the 1970's downswing of OEO and the concurrent upswing of the Office of Minority Business Enterprise (OMBE —U.S. Department of Commerce) and its related Minority Enterprise Small Business Investment Corporation (MESBIC —Small Business Administration) Program, many shifts in funding and program thrusts have occurred throughout the South.

The Federation of Southern Cooperatives, for example, has shifted from the Ford Foundation and OEO as their prime funding sources to OMBE. Moreover, the entire OEO (currently Community Services Administration) Title VII program continues to be subject to imminent transfer to OMBE.[34]

The OEO and OMBE Program concepts are quite different in their thrusts and orientation:

Program Concept Comparison[35]

Title VII—OEO *Community Economic Development*	OMBE *Minority Entrepreneurship*
1. The focus is on *a low-income community*.	1. The focus is on an economically or socially disadvantaged *individual*.

2. Strategic answers include:
   A. Better planning, coordination, mobilization, integration of existing resources.
   B. Creation of new, or expansion of existing resources, including: *Social Tools* (institutions), *Human Resources, Physical Resources,* and *Flexible Equity Capital.*
   C. Ownership by the community.
3. Measures of program success include:
   A. Number of new institutions (viable business and other)
   B. Greater diversification of institutional opportunities
   C. Increase in incomes of residents
   D. Increased employment in upgraded jobs
   E. Incomes increase for lower ranges
   F. Upgraded physical environment to increase community attraction
   G. Stability or increase in net immigration of talent and skills
   H. Increased investments, especially equity investments of residents.

2. Strategic answers include:
   A. Greater personal skills in management, accounting, marketing, etc.
   B. Access to technical assistance, consultation to gain access to *Debt Capital* and *Markets.*
   C. Ownership by the entrepreneur.
3. Program success is measured in one way: Does the citizen now own and operate a viable business (or larger scale business)?

During this same period, nine MESBICs (Minority Enterprise Small Business Investment Corporations) have been licensed to operate in the Deep South and parts of Appalachia,[36] including a seven-state MESBIC operating as a part of the Southern Cooperative Development Fund and Equal Opportunity Finance, serving Kentucky, West Virginia, and part of Ohio in Appalachia.[37]

Other Influences of the 1970's

General Revenue Sharing, a part of the Nixon administration's answer to establishing a "new federalism"—a move which would give more funds, and hence power, back to state and local government control—has been a crushing disappointment to rural community leaders. General Revenue Sharing has not provided any funds to establish or continue legitimate self-help efforts. Most rural counties in Appalachia and the Deep South received only enough funding, under General Revenue Sharing, to buy a bulldozer or road grader, and that is precisely how many of the tax-impoverished county governments used their share.

Even in southern urban areas where significantly more funds were available, very little has been invested in community social or economic programs of any kind. For example, the Knoxville, Tennessee, city council turned down a strongly-supported citizen proposal to use ½ of 1% of their General Revenue Sharing funds for social programs, opting instead for street and city facility construction and improvement.

Special Revenue Sharing, on the other hand, has been supposedly designed to meet the community social and economic needs so badly missed by General Revenue Sharing. Currently, Special Revenue Sharing is the consolidation of a number of federal categorical programs into four broad areas: community development, education, manpower training, and law enforcement.

The community development program—the area most likely to affect low income cooperatives (LICs) and other community economic and social efforts in the South—has been legislated into being through the Housing and Community Development Act of 1974. However, thus far its thrust has been predominately urban in setting, and brick and mortar in character.

Moreover, the new Manpower Training Act taking effect in 1974 has done little to make training funds accessible to LICs. As these and other aspects of Special Revenue Sharing, yet to be legislated, are considered, the thought-nagging question remains: What share of revenue can an LIC in rural county, South, expect from any Revenue Sharing Act once it is passed?

The frustrating but realistic answer seems to come back—
nothing! In reality, both revenue sharing programs seem to be
part of a conscious or unconscious effort to undo all past progress toward social and economic justice which has been won, at
such a high cost, over the past several decades. Power is not
being returned to the low income people, or the ordinary citizen, but rather to the very officials whose disregard for the
rights, needs, and desires of the poor prompted federal poverty
programs, social services, and civil rights legislation in the
first place.[38]

The Rural Development Act of 1972 has been another disappointment to rural CED and social leaders. A disappointment in both the sense that the original thrust of the bill
has been blunted by airtight regulations which shoot over
the heads of most local community groups—control being
vested in the federal political system and a high level state
committee headed by the governor—and by the fact that it
took more than a year after its enactment before any funds
were spent under its new authority.

In 1973 Senator Dick Clark, Chairman of the Senate Subcommittee on Rural Development, had commented that "over
the year since the passage of the Rural Development Act,
rather than making progress, we have gone backwards in
meeting the needs of rural America."[39]

The Nixon administration did implement the RDA loan
authorities in its F.Y. 1974 budget. However, the funding of grant programs has been sharply curtailed. Such grant
programs, in any case, are not available to LICs or non-
profit corporations. The legislation and insuing regulations
specify that only "units of government," with a tax base,
are eligible for grants under RDA authority. Moreover, even
though RDA loan programs may be funded, their usefulness
for LICs and community-based business ventures appears
quite limited, since the lending authority is limited to 90%
guarantees of conventional bank loans, a condition which
capital-starved rural banks and groups will find hard to meet.

The proposed regulations also defer to current Small Business Administration programs (such as 502 Local Development Corporation and Economic Opportunity Loans) and the lending activities of local banks setting out the role of RDA financing as that of a Guarantor of Bank Loans for ventures too large for SBA to handle.[40]

On a more positive side, the 1970's have currently brought the potential for more technical assistance from at least one government agency, a liberalized loan program from the *Small Business Administration*, and a new outlook by one government agency directly affecting Appalachia toward the encouragement of entrepreneurship.

In the area of technical assistance, the *Economic Development Administration* has been granted additional funds for technical help. This help, in the past, has proved most useful to community groups. However, this increase is targeted primarily toward communities affected by closings and cutbacks in military installations, Indian tribes, and communities which need assistance in relation to Rural Development Act loans.

The *Small Business Administration* has Economic Opportunity Loans available, in amounts up to $50,000, for any co-op which might choose to separate its processing or marketing function from production and incorporate that function as a for-profit entity. SBA also has 502 loans, in amounts up to $350,000, for groups which have or can organize a Local Development Company (LDC) and direct the loan to a specific for-profit business.

Finally, the *Appalachian Regional Commission*—the federal agency charged with primary responsibility in the development of the Central Sub-Region of Appalachia—is currently exploring the use of ARC funds to encourage entrepreneural development in the region in addition to their more traditional, but marginally successful, role of encouraging industrial immigration. The encouragement of individual or group entrepreneurship is a new type of developmental emphasis for ARC. But, evidently, the commission feels it must become more directly involved in the creation of jobs and the stimulation of private enterprises and "generic" industries.[41]

Directions for the Future

As Al Ulmer, then with the Southern Regional Council, put it in 1969, "Realistic hopes for rural co-ops are (still) linked inescapably with the hope for reconstruction of the rural South."[42] However, as Ulmer relates, many co-ops have become, since the 1960's, more than "holding actions or 'demonstration' programs . . . making it possible for a few people to stay in the rural South who otherwise would have no alternative but to starve or migrate."[43]

LICs have grown or perished in the lean years since 1970. The survivors have expanded both horizontally and vertically. They have become more economically and politically sophisticated and have set off a multiplier effect in many communities—an effect which Marshall and Godwin prophesied.[44] This has stimulated action by public and private agencies and local and state governments and started, at least, a process—a beginning—toward the renewal of the rural South for *all* its citizens.

Nevertheless, much remains to be done. The summary of the Abt study states:

> The findings of the study indicate that the cooperative can effectively provide benefits to people bypassed by the major rural development strategies. It can become a viable institution, and thus continue to provide benefits without outside support. The implementation of cooperative support policy under existing or new legislation is recommended.[45]

Yet such existing legislation, which could reinforce existing LICs and make the development of new ones possible, remains unfunded, unenforced, or regulated out of business. New legislation, with all its liberal intentions, invariably misses the mark at the local level, and the people's struggle for self-determination continues with very little *real* assistance from our government.

The church's role in this struggle seems clear-cut; we must support, in whatever way we can—politically, economically, technically—the realization of human dignity found in true cooperation, *the little people's chance in a world of bigness.* What one young minister wrote about his native Appalachia could also be written of the total cooperative movement among the rural poor:

> Our challenge is not to join mainstream America. It is to re-create a renewed and authentic form of what the mountains have always been. From the time that the first white settlers deliberately cut their ties with the coastal culture of colonial America to start a new life in this wilderness, the mountains have offered an alternative to mainstream America. . . . The task before us is to renew this alternative and endow it with the capabilities (including an adequate economic base) it will need to survive the late twentieth century America.[46]

PART II
The "Why":
Economic Development
as Christian Mission

Bread for Life:
The Churches and
Rural Economic Development

DONALD W. SHRIVER, JR.

Theologians are under great pressure from churchmen and others today to be "relevant." One response to that pressure has been the proliferation of what has been called "genitive theologies," theologies *of* something. Thus we get theologies of sex, of environment, of war, of technology, and of development. The danger in this proliferation is just the danger faced by the early Hebrew prophets in their struggle with Baalism, which could well be called the Canaanite theology of economic development. *Agricultural fertility* was the divinity of ultimate concern in this religion. You paid your respects to the *baalim* of the land because you wanted food, prosperity, and abundance of children. Baalism was a man-centered religion; its gods were resident in the lands and fields; and the aim of its religious ritual was to keep these gods satisfied and healthy.

The Hebrew prophets condemned Baalism and the worship of all other "gods" which were human needs in disguise. The God of Abraham, Isaac, and Jacob was concerned about their needs, but he could never be reduced to those concerns. "If your real god is your stomach,"—Moses had reason to say on more than one occasion to his ragged followers—"you should have stayed in Egypt!" In the historical adventure which the God of Abraham calls his people to undertake, no particular human good must be mistaken for the one great good of fidelity to the Lord himself, who is always introducing his people to a richer *range* of good things than they have yet encountered in their experience. All through the Old Testament and into the New, there is a mysterious,

49

still-to-be-appropriated "blessing" in the covenant loyalty of a chosen people to their covenanting Lord. And when all the blessings of earthly life are added up, they do not total the sheer blessedness of fellowship with the great and the loving Creator!

It is against this Old Testament background that we can understand the two major dimensions of the "economic thinking" of Jesus. He obviously did a lot of thinking about economic questions. His teachings are full of references to sowing and reaping, building and investing, pearls and coins, wealthy people and poor people. No easy summary of all these teachings is possible, but a basic pair of principles seemed to run straight through all he said and did: (1) man's Lord and Creator, not bread, is the totality of human fulfillment, (2) but bread is basic to that fulfillment.

"Man cannot live on bread alone; he lives on every word that God utters." (Matt. 4:4 N.E.B.) Jesus said this in a moment when he was in the clutch of the economic problem in its rawest human form: he was acutely hungry. He had forty days before been baptized by John. The context suggests that John and others already saw him as an extraordinary person. In his whole ministry someone would always be close at hand to call him a "superman." That is one way to interpret all three of the temptations which beset him just after the baptism: was he going to spend the next several years *dominating* other people or identifying with them? At stake, the temptation story implies, is the very nature of God, man, and the God-man relationship. Does God delight most in being over man or in being with him? Should a man's ambition be to be superior to his neighbors or to be one with them in utter equality? At stake, in short, is the reality of the incarnation, whether or not in Jesus God identifies himself with humanity. If he does, then he cannot resort to getting bread for himself through the special pull of miracle! He must resort to the same place that every other man gets his bread: the grain market and the grocery store! This is the spiritual victory of Jesus' successful resistance of the first temptation: he opts for common rather than extraordinary humanity. He continues to act, as he did in his baptism and as he will in his death, as brother to the rest of us. And in that, he lays the ground of the insistence of John's Gospel and the Nicene Creed that in Jesus Christ God "became flesh."

Of great moment here is the place of *neighborliness* in the definition of human nature. Had Jesus chosen to act like the hero of liberal economic philosophy—"let every man pursue his self-interest first"—he would have yielded blithely to the temptation. And if he had yielded, he would have furnished Marxists with a great proof-text of their own theory of human nature: that man does live by bread alone, that the economic question is *the* question of human life. No, says Jesus, *the* question is the theological question: As men to whom are we ultimately loyal? And does that ultimate loyalty produce in its adherents a profound loyalty to each other's welfare—does it yield an ethic?

It is worth noting that much of the discussion of "development" in the so-called developing countries hinges on a kindred issue. Both the Marxists and the capitalists are having trouble peddling their philosophy in some of these countries, precisely because the two seem to agree that *economic* development is the only important form of *human* development. Not so, say the leaders of countries like Tanzania: "Freedom from colonialism and the preservation of some of our local traditions are at least as important as the accumulation of western-style wealth. It is more important to us to be human than merely to be rich!" That is a clear echo of Jesus' own teaching that "a man's life does not consist of the abundance of things which he possesses." The same truth glimmers in our own experience of knowing some rich people whose humanity seems shriveled and some poor people who are wonderfully, almost miraculously human. Any person—like many a pastor and social worker—who has been privileged to know a number of really poor people knows that on occasion they display a humility, a grace, and a sense of humor which puts some of their prosperous neighbors to shame. Neither in the Christian perspective nor in much of our ordinary experience is it true that "man lives by bread *alone*." The measure of human life is more complex and profound than the measure of a full pantry.

Yet the experience of knowing poor people also suggests the other pole of Jesus' own thinking about bread: If bread were not so important to a fully human life, the chance to get bread by "passing a miracle" would not have been so *tempting* to Jesus. He knew that man does live by bread, even though he had to establish the prior principle that he does not live by bread alone. The old theologians would have said that bread is a "necessary but not sufficient cause" of the fully human life. The statistics on brain-damage among malnourished children are grim reminders of that. Jesus put it simply and directly in a prayer that appears in the Gospel of Matthew just two chapters away from the temptation story: "Give us this day our daily bread."

The first section of the Lord's Prayer is the very embodiment of the chief victory in the temptation: God's name, kingdom, and will are of first importance in the lives of his creatures. But when the creature of this Creator turns to his own human needs, he boldly puts "daily bread" at the head of the list. The simplicity and the concreteness of the petition for bread, on the lips of Jesus and on the lips of millions of Christians who have repeated the prayer after him, suggest that *economic* questions have been *central* to the theology and ethics of the church from the very beginning of church history. Notably enough, in asking for bread we ask for an object that is both a creation of God and a fabrication of man. In so asking, Jesus and his followers are counting on the fact that the Father in heaven is not only lord of the natural order (like the lords of the Canaanites) but is lord over human history, including human economic systems. We hope not only that he may give the world good crops but that he may give us *bread*—that he may not camp merely on the perimeter of our marketing systems but may be present where bread is baked, where its price is fixed, and in all the exchanges whereby bread finally reaches *hungry human mouths*.

The word "our" is used nine times in the Lord's Prayer. No person is expected to pray "like this" (Matt. 6:9) outside the physical or the implied presence of other people. It is the same spiritual reality that triumphed in the temptation: man does not eat bread in loneliness! Eating is a social occasion par excellence, beginning with the family and extending to the whole human community. Indeed, the word "our" in the Lord's Prayer is fraternal and intercessional towards the whole of humanity. Who can imagine Jesus praying that God would give some special attention to the needs of his followers for bread? Our need for bread is exactly like that of our human neighbors the world around; and as Christians we are to yearn for bread *for them* as earnestly as we yearn for it for ourselves. This yearning is a part of that universal groaning which Paul describes in the eighth chapter of Romans: "We ourselves, who have the first fruits of the Spirit, groan inwardly as we wait for adoption as sons, the redemption of our bodies." (Rom. 8:23) A more glorious "redemption of our bodies" is anticipated for man here than the glory of health and vitality for our old physical bodies; but it is in accord with the eschatology of both testaments to say that anything that ministers to the health of our present bodies is an early "downpayment" on the salvation that God ultimately intends for his people. Indeed, the Biblical vision of "salvation" is notable for the number of *materialistic* images that are freely resorted to by writers as different as Jeremiah and Paul. In Jeremiah 32 the prophet sees the future salvation of his people in terms of the restoration of "houses and fields and vineyards" to the Babylon-ravaged land; and Paul, on the basis of his faith in the resurrection of Jesus, envisions a future for man that will have *body* to it and the full "fruits" of the Spirit. As William Temple said, "Christianity is the most . . . materialist of all the great religions." Those who believe in the incarnation are driven to such a conclusion. If "God was in Christ," *in* a real man with a real physical body, how very *important* the human body becomes! And how very consistent is the incarnational theology by which Jesus previewed the judgment of the whole human race at the end of history: "Inasmuch as you gave food, drink, hospitality, clothes, and a simple visit to the least of these my brethren, you did these things to me." (from Matthew 25:31-44)

In the face of all that, how did the Christian church ever acquire modern day members who say to each other: "The church should stick to spiritual matters, and stay out of all these political and economic affairs!"? If God took the realm of economics so seriously as to subject himself in Jesus to the human need for bread, and if the meaning of that incarnation is that *every* man's need for bread has the force of God's claim to our attention, there is no *Christian* way to ignore economic questions!

Fortunately we live in a time when churchmen around the world are rediscovering the imperatives of "social questions" as they grow out of the gospel and as they relate to the events of our history. And poor, hungry people around the world, so long used to an economy of scarcity, are coming to realize that gross poverty is not inevitable for the majority of humankind. With the new tools of technology at hand, the "revolution of rising expectations" has swept almost every human tribe on the globe. One can interpret this revolution in terms of psychology and politics alone if one wants; but against the background of a close reading of the Bible, the Christian will be inclined to see it all as part of God's work in history.

In sum: As the churches join with other institutions to implement the world-wide human yearning that bread be justly distributed to all human mouths, part of our task will be to witness to the insufficiency of "bread alone" as the fulfillment of humanity. It will also be our task to witness to the priority of "bread for us" over "bread for me." These are the two basic ingredients of a Christian ethic for economic affairs to be derived from the teachings of Jesus.

General theological principles like the above will be brought by Christians to their consideration of the subject of economic development. Such principles are part of the yardstick against which God himself means to measure all human economic systems in all times. Like Amos' plumb line, these principles hang straight from God's hand down the profile of economic systems of every age, revealing their crookedness and injustices (Amos 7: 7-8). As such, our knowledge of "what the Lord requires of us" has a consistency from age to age, a certain solidity and independence which keeps us from thinking that God's yardsticks change as often as our economic systems change.

But on the other side of all this generality is the truth that like other men we Christians have much to learn about the programs and systems by which men in the twentieth and twenty-first centuries may achieve unprecedented levels of economic justice. The problem of getting more bread into the mouths of hungry children on the tenant farms of South Georgia, for example, is not to be solved by a close reading of the Bible alone. One may have to read also just as closely the most recent government farm legislation and the most recent techniques for the organization of farm labor unions! Indeed, in recent years certain leaders in the major church denominations of this country have given evidence of formulating programs which bear the imprint of both sorts of close reading: the reading of the Bible and the reading of the current social scene in combination. These leaders are saying to the churches that in our current society there are new handles for the church to grasp for practical ministry to the economic needs of poor people. Such a set of new handles was recommended recently by the Southeastern Jurisdictional Council of the United Methodist Church in its 1971 statement, "Economic Development as Christian Mission." The key paragraph in the statement was:

> In view of the limited resources of the churches . . . we believe that we must be selective in choosing those forms of economic development which are most in line with our basic Christian assumptions. To this end, we commit our highest

priority in the field of economic development to the support of community-based, cooperative, self-help forms of economic enterprise.

I cannot be sure just what basic Christian assumptions lay behind the Council's choice of three emphases in the program policy recommended here—"community-based, cooperative, self-help"—but these three terms have the marks of both Christian tradition and social modernity. It is appropriate, I think, to consider how the Christian and the modern elements may be linked and to probe the combination of the ancient and the modern in the statement, if only to underscore the importance of a style of churchmanship that comports very well with the famous recommendation of Karl Barth: that Christians live their lives "with the Bible in one hand and the newspaper in the other." It is not enough in the Christian life to know something about God's plumb line for the judgment of the world; it is also necessary to work at the job of making the walls straighter, specifically corrected in certain times and places. One may rightly end these "theological reflections" therefore by looking at the specifics in terms of the above Biblical background and the foreground of the contemporary American economy.

Community-Based Development

The first element in this proposed church-supported program for economic development concerns what and who are to be developed : the economic resources of a *group* of people.

This element corresponds very closely to the term *our* in the Lord's Prayer. It flies in the face of one of the major presuppositions of the economic liberalism associated with the name Adam Smith and associated as well with the economic development of the United States. Smith, who wrote his classic *The Wealth of Nations* (a wonderful coincidence) in the year 1776, was an economic liberal in the sense that he believed in a "free" market, carried on among "free" individuals who acted "rationally" in terms of the promotion of their own self-interest individually. That is, the market in Smith's analysis was composed of atomic individuals, not corporate communities. His theory was partly a reaction to mercantile policy in Britain, whose leaders sought to promote the interests of the home country at the expense of all its colonies and trading partners. It was in America that the liberal economic philosophy had its first test on a huge scale. As historians remind us, seldom in human history has any nation been founded by so many persons who were eager to act just as Adam Smith said they should act: as self-interested, autonomous individuals whose chief aim in life was to maximixe their own wealth. "Go West, young man!" Horace Greeley advised Easterners, who took his advice in droves. It was the thirst for wealth, and an almost holy hatred of poverty, that accounts for the wanderlust of many an American.

All of this says that the typical American does not think much in terms of "community-based" economic development. At most he believes in economic development "for my family." To be sure, some of the settlers of this country came with a vision of a community. First the Puritans, and then a stream of communitarian groups like the Amish and the Owenites, came determined to build "cities set on a hill." The Puritans, in particular, had a vision of a New Community, bound together by common laws and obligations. But the New England Puritans rapidly developed a spirit for economic individualism that turned them into the proverbial Yankees. The difference between the Puritan and the Yankee was that the Puritan thought of himself first as a member of a community, while the Yankee thought of himself first as an individual who had economic dealings with the community. For the latter, the individual was the "real man." In this sense the Puritan was closer to the thought-world of the Bible; and in this same sense, the traditions of many rural parts of America, especially the South, are closer to that same thought-world.

It is dangerous to suggest that rural America, or the rural south, has particular affinity to the world of the Bible; for, among other things, rural America is only too dominated by individualistic, Yankee-like farmers. But underlying this, especially in the South, there is a sense of community that is sometimes lacking in urban America. James McBride Dabbs used to say that this sense of community was one of the signs that southern society was "haunted by God." God wills men to live together, each loving his neighbor as persons like himself, and at their best southerners still define themselves in terms of neighborly ties. "Where are you from?" the southerner will frequently ask a stranger. The more typical Yankee question would be, "What do you do for a living?" In the South we want to know what a stranger's human associations are, what local dirt still hangs on the roots of his life, even after he has pulled up those roots and moved to a new place. We do not know who the man really *is* until we know who are his most intimate community associates.

That real men are developed, not atomically as units, but collectively in communities, is an insight dawning in many an American mind in the early 1970's. Everywhere we hear murmurs of uneasiness over the inhuman sundering of one person from association with another in an economy that moves men around from job to job, separates old people from their children, and destroys friendships in the name of economic opportunity. Many a rural county in the South is steadily losing its young people to the lure of "good jobs" in the cities; and the economy of the countryside is steadily being reorganized into "agribusiness," which is primarily concerned not with the preservation or development of community ties but with profit to faraway stockholders. Not everything that agribusiness does to reorganize the rural economy is bad for the local community, of course; but some agribusiness policy is bound to be humanly callous if it lets stock-holder profit be the primary value of rural enterprise. *There is need in the rural areas for organized economic development that puts the preservation and development of the community itself high rather than low in the priority list;*

and the churches are beginning to see this need as one mandate of its own particular mission. And along with some leaders in government, some church leaders are beginning to recognize that there is no hope for the development of true human community in the cities of America apart from some new stability and health in the country's rural areas. Most especially this applies to the need to make it possible for the most desperately poor people of the countryside to find economic salvation where they are, rather than to look for it—in vain, mostly—in the ghettos of the big city.

A postscript to this point is especially pertinent to the South: When James Dabbs said that he felt God haunting the South, he referred particularly to the central social question of southern history: whether, and to what degree, black people and white people belong to the *same* social community. Our institutions, beginning with slavery, said Dabbs, tell us that the two races are two peoples; but our "unofficial" experience of community with each other tell us that we are one people. Certainly the Bible—in spite of some tortured exegesis among some southern theologians—has been telling us all along that we are one people. Now the federal government has been telling us that, too. And economic fact seems to tell us that increasingly—for the problems of the poor white person and the poor black person in the South are almost exactly the same problem. It would be a curious economic development program in most southern rural communities that ignored the interdependence of white people and black people there. For very practical, temporary reasons it may be necessary on occasion to have a "white economic development program" and a "black economic development program"; but the church should be clear-minded about the economic and the theological inadequacy of such programs in the long run. Neither God nor hunger is a respecter of skin color!

Cooperative Economic Development

The word "cooperative" in the Methodist policy statement bears overtones of a very specific form of economic organization, largely invented during the past hundred years but having its roots far back in history in many forms, including the early Christian experiment in economic sharing. In its modern form, the cooperative is a compromise between the business corporation and large scale socialism. It is typically a community economic enterprise—a cannery, a sawmill, or an electric power system—whose ownership, governance, and profit belong to all of its members. When they grow to include a very large number of members, cooperatives can behave much like business corporations; but when organized around the interests of a relatively small community—like a hundred cattle farmers—they are likely to be effective instruments for developing and preserving a local community.

The moral superiority of the cooperative idea over the usual stock-company idea stems from its initial impetus in the question, "How can we best improve each other's prosperity in terms of our shared interests?" Individual profit is often the only criterion invoked for an investor's decision to put money in a stock company. In effect, the cooperative idea calls for the ethical judgment that *economic cooperation takes priority over economic competition.* Economics begins with the problems of a group of people considered in their togetherness, rather than considered in their separation from each other. Not that competition has no place in achieving some benefit for large numbers of people, e.g., in keeping prices lower than they might otherwise be. But competition is not the unalloyed human good that some capitalist theorists claim it to be. Look in any rural or urban ghetto, and you will see the casualties of the competitive system: the people who for one reason or another were left behind in the great American race for wealth. As likely as not, they were left behind from the moment of their birth—think again of the obvious, gross illustration of the malnourished child in an impoverished county, who gnaws at clay and leaves, and who thus begins life crippled in brain and body. As Michael Harrington said ten years ago, the biggest "mistake" the poor make is being born poor. Forever after that, the statistics are not on your side in the United States.

If the Christian churches did not invent cooperatives, they have in their own history some precedents for understanding and appreciating the *political* aspect of the cooperative idea. When Cesar Chavez organized the farm workers of California, he was acting politically as well as economically. If they really mean to achieve changes in an unjust economic system, poor people must band together. Sometimes their only strength is their numbers. This is the principle of labor unionism, of course. And surprisingly enough to some individualistic Christians, there is precedent in church history for the idea of unionism. Historians tell us that John Wesley's preaching of the gospel in the coal fields of western Britain resulted in the organization of hundreds of Methodist chapels, which were subdivided into thousands of small "classes" of about a dozen persons each. In these chapels and classes, some coal miners had their first experience of organizing and leading a social group outside of their own families. Here they began to understand how men get things done in groups; and many an early leader of the British labor movement got his political training in this way. An almost parallel story could be told of the black church in America, which has been the one organization in the black community that black people controlled and which, in the 1960's, provided a base for the organization of the civil rights movement.

These illustrations go far to suggest that the old claim that "religion and politics don't mix" has never been historically accurate. The two are not the *same*, but they are invariably *related*, and what church people have to decide is their difference between a humanly *good* and a humanly *bad* relationship between religion and politics. A church that stands idly by and sees the mechanical cotton-picker deprive thousands of sharecroppers of their jobs, while the owners of the cotton plantation make hundreds of thousands of dollars from a government farm program, is a supporter of a bad mixture of religion and politics! But a church that springs to the aid of those sharecroppers, sets up the Mississippi Delta Ministry, and helps the victims of injustice to unite in their own interest is more likely to be a supporter of a good mixture. The sum of it all is that the Martin Luther Kings, the Cesar Chavezes and other organizers of the poor are more the friends of the Christian movement than some of its prosperous members have had the humility to recognize. (I am one of those prosperous members, so I say this repentently. It is easy when you are well-fed to forget the reality of hunger in your neighbor. Sometimes he has to remind you of that hunger by cutting off your supply of lettuce or picketing the place you buy groceries.)

It is a repetitive footnote, but it bears repeating: just as the community of the poor in the South includes whites and blacks, cooperation for economic development must include them too. Not so long ago on the Gulf Coast in Alabama a woodcutter's union was organized by white and black people, a relatively unprecedented thing in the South. If Christians know their theology and their economics, they will pray for the increase of such ventures—for the Koinonia Farms, the Penn Community Centers, and other such cracks in the segregated economic structure. Put it down as almost undisputable practical wisdom: both Christian ethics and modern economics call for the abolition of racism as a principle for organizing people in an economic enterprise.

Self-Help Forms of Enterprise

Theologically and ethically, as a Christian, I like the order in which the Methodist Council put those three adjectives: community-based, cooperative, self-help. The order suggests that the community and the cooperation are the context for the self-help. Indeed, the "self" here might be a community, a group of people.

Unless this context is understood, the idea of "self-help" can be easily misunderstood—both theologically and economically. The notion of self-help is very prominent in liberal economic theory: "God helps those who help themselves," proclaims this theory proudly. Too many people in America think of this motto as coming from the Bible. Look through a thousand pages, and you will not find these words in the Bible. In fact, you will find some quite different words like: "By grace you have been saved through faith; and this is not your own doing, it is the gift of God—not because of works, lest any man should boast." (Ephesians 2: 8-9) The Bible is not the place to support the idea of the "self-made man," no matter how much American culture may celebrate that ideal. In so many ordinary ways it is possible to debunk that ideal. Psychology and sociology have made us abundantly aware that every individual person moves into life trailing clouds of debts to other persons. For everything we achieve on our own there is something somebody else achieved for us. And if Jesus is our supreme guide in the matter, we must remember that his greatness did not consist in his ability to help himself, but in his ability to trust in the help of God the Father. The crucifixion and the resurrection are our final demonstration of that.

To this great overriding Christian reason for qualifying the idea of "self-help" must be added the facts of social life in our time. The worldwide human community is getting more interdependent all the time. The economy of one nation impinges upon the economy of others. The economic problems of the city and the countryside grow in proportion to one another; and the economic development of one requires the economic development of the other. The rise of agribusiness and government farm programs demonstrates this; and however much such programs need to be delivered of their injustices, we are unlikely to return in this country to a nation of small farmers or small communities who can work out their economic destinies unilaterally and uncooperatively.

Having said all this, one can return to the wisdom of "self-help" programs for improving the economic lot of the poor in rural areas. *The issue here is the need for more dignity and less paternalism in the relations of the rich and the poor people of all societies.* In economic development, what is to be de-

veloped is not only a material product but the *capacities* of
the human producers. Human development is the goal, not
merely economic development. We know that one of the
characteristics of a fully developed human being is an ability
to *initiate* projects for his own and other people's betterment.
A human being who is always passively waiting for other
people to do things for him is not a fully developed human
being. Given the choice between creating a certain amount of
wealth *for* people and enabling *them* to create it, modern
economic developers will always choose the latter. That is
one painful lesson of some of the missionary programs of our
churches and some of the economic aid programs of our
governments: It turns out that man does not live by bread
alone; he lives also in the dignity and freedom of helping to
create his own future. Thus, leaders like Julius Nyerere of
Tanzania are saying to development-minded people outside
his country that self-development is as important to Tanzan-
ians as development itself. "We'll turn down your offers of
investment capital," he says in effect, "and we will achieve
economic growth at a slower rate, if that is the price we must
pay for remaining in control of our own futures. We do not
want our lives managed merely according to rates of return
on your investments, even if we ourselves acquired more
money in the process. For such a process would make us poorer
human beings by depriving us of dignity and self-direction."

The upshot of this is that, even if it could be proved that
rich powerful people know what is "best" for poor weak
people, it is better for the latter on their own to say what is
best, because only in this way will they begin to acquire
power of their own. Such a principle does not deny the importance of the other principles—community and cooperation.
Rather, it helps define the kind of community and cooperation which we all need around us: not the kind that suffocates
us with gifts but which liberates us with opportunity, variety,
and invitation to inventiveness. As a matter of fact, do the
rich of the world really know what is good for the poor of
the world? The rich know little enough what is good for

themselves! How much the poor may have to teach the rich about the art of being human: for example, how to suffer privation with aplomb. Many of us in our affluence must confess that the poor have taught us more than we have ever taught them. Indeed it is a prejudice peculiarly widespread in America that material wealth is somehow synonymous with wisdom and ability, not to speak of happiness. That idea is clearly implied in one of the best-known, most anti-Christian mottoes ever to hang over a bar in these United States: "If you're so smart, why ain't you rich?" Someday the judge of all the earth will hang that one in the balance of his judgment upon "the nations" (Matt. 25:32); and he will say to those who put up such signs the devastating word: "You forgot that *I* was poor!" It's basic theology: God helps the poor, enabling them to help themselves.

Indeed, the rich are so likely to forget the poor, including the poverty of a man named Jesus, that we can well understand how in the Bible God is frequently identified as the one who "remembers the poor." Who else but God can be counted on to remember them? That, at least, is the conclusion to which many a poor man has been driven in societies ancient and modern. God is on the side of the poor when all the human power and prestige is arrayed on the other side. If the poor did not have that sort of faith, how would one account for their extraordinary persistence? As Robert Coles said in a newspaper interview not long ago, in his exposure to hundreds of poor people he finds little evidence that religion functions as a Marxian "opiate of the people," dulling their drive for social justice here and now. Quite the contrary, said Coles: Religious faith is a source of hope and courage which enables the poor to "voice all kinds of revolutionary passions which might otherwise go unexpressed." I myself have known poor men and women who have suffered blows and tragedies which would drive other human beings to suicide. Instead, they "keep on keeping on," stubbornly hopeful like the Psalmist who cried: "I believe that I shall see the goodness of the LORD in the land of the living! Wait for the LORD: be strong, and let your heart take courage. . . ." (Ps. 27:13-14)

It is the business of the church to see that the poor of the earth do not wait so long that their only recourse is to the *last* judgment of God. If we and they wait that long, the poor will be vindicated finally, but rich men will not. And since the churches of America in particular are filled with so many of us who are comparatively very rich, a great burden of responsibility falls upon the church. The dignity and the humanity of the poor requires that they participate in their own march to economic justice; but the tools, the skills, and the social system changes for that self-help must come partly through the help of others. As never before in history, men as a whole have it in their power to make almost every land on earth a "land flowing with milk and honey." The God of creation, judgment, and redemption seems at work in our world to make it so. But he will make it so with the help of men who love their neighbors enough to be concerned with such concrete economic affairs as the buying of land, the pasturing of milk cows, and the raising of honey bees! The church is called to concern itself with economic development in just this concreteness. In our time, that is one of our ways for preaching good news to the poor. Anything less will not be heard by them as good enough.

Theology for the Wretched
of the Earth

HAL M. WAREHIME

*"Again I saw all the oppressions that are practiced under
the sun. And behold, the tears of the oppressed, and they
had no one to comfort them! On the side of their oppressors
there was power, and there was no one to comfort them."*
Ecclesiastes 4:1

*"Then the Lord said, 'I have seen the affliction of my peo-
ple . . . and have heard their cry because of their taskmasters;
I know their sufferings, and I have come down to deliver
them . . . and to bring them out . . . to a good and broad
land, a land flowing with milk and honey. . . . Come, I will
send you to Pharoah that you may bring forth my people . . .
out of Egypt.'"*
Exodus 3:7-10

*"'Truly, I say to you, as you did it to one of the least of
these my brethren, you did it to me.'"*
Matthew 25:40

Note: Some of the people whom I had in mind as I wrote this
article, and whose presence there served as a source
and selector of ideas, are:

R., An impecunious woman who slavishly served the country-
club rich for "pennies" and who died "all wore out" at the
age of 47.

H., One of the millions of blacks whose coerced and unrewarded labor created the capital for white America's
prosperity.

J., A miner in eastern Kentucky whose life was spent underground, whose lungs are filled with dirt, and whose every attempt to organize his colleagues was broken by a powerful operator's association.

B., An illiterate Chicano child whose "stoop labor" from dawn to dark in the lettuce fields of Arizona produces profits to send the grower's son to Harvard.

S., A Jew who went too lamblike into the fiery furnace of Auschwitz.

G., A student from a dispossessed minority group sinking deeper and deeper in debt, who was legally charged 31% interest on a loan from a finance company.

L., The drunken remains of a "noble savage" on an Indian reservation whose ancestors trusted greedy white men "not wisely, but too well."

M., A bank teller with three children, unhappy with her work and her wages, who dares not search for another job for fear that her employer will find it out and fire her as he has done in similar cases.

C., An old black woman, crazy with the worries of poverty and powerlessness, who shouts poignant praises to Jesus for blessings she never receives.

T., A Mexican peasant, one of the world's majority who, "with God's help" and the Church's blessing, is starving to death.

Salvation = Bread

The earth is presently populated by masses of wretched people, and the major cause of their misery is a desperate want of Bread: the just political and economic developments that can serve to glue a human body and soul together for a long and honorable life.

Such people are the world's majority. They can be found in every nation and almost every neighborhood of the earth.

They are dramatically and realistically symbolized by the little man with a shrunken belly who died of starvation recently near the doorstep of an affluent clergyman.[1] Their need for Bread is the most urgent item on the modern world's agenda, and the survival and fate of all of us hangs on how soon and how well the need is dealt with.

All religions, and particularly the Christian religion and its churches, have always claimed to be preeminently concerned about the salvation of the world. It is, therefore, appropriate and timely to inquire about the special contribution which Christianity might make to this situation which calls urgently for the salvaging of the wretched millions of hungry humans on this planet.

It is the position of this piece that *the least* Christianity may supply to help redeem the world is a type of theology which inspires, supports, and justifies the kinds of political action and economic developments that can put fresh flesh on dry bones and breathe new life into desperate spirits. A theology which does anything less or other than this will contribute to the persistence of the problem, not its solution.

What might be some of the marks of such a theology?

Sources: Empty Stomachs and Visions of Justice

First of all, a Christian theology for the wretched of the earth must be intimately informed and supremely influenced by two main sources. The first and the more important source is the *experiences of wretchedness* which are common to millions of mankind. Here is where this theology must start: not with the experiences of affluence in Middle America and its problems of anxiety, ennui, and anomie where so much modern theology begins and the churches' ministry too often ends, but with the experiences of threatened physical survival and desperate social impotence in the Other Americas of the world and their frustrated needs for food, power, and pride. An authentic theology for these people will take seriously, as its primary data, empty stomachs, illiterate minds, diseased bodies, unrewarded labor, flat purses, enslaving debts, puppet governments, war-ravaged villages, plundered resources, and premature death. In short, this theology must deal with the common demonic fact of socio-economic injustice and its consequences of wasted human lives, because in a world where some people must diet, it is unjust that many other people starve, and in a world where many are helpless, it is unjust that some have power to abuse.

The second main source which must inform and influence this theology is the *prophetic tradition* of the Bible and the church. This source contains the work and words of men such as Moses, Amos, Isaiah, Jesus, Maurice, Rauschenbusch, Niebuhr, and King. It is a tradition which takes human wretchedness and social injustice in this world with the utmost seriousness. It worships a God of history who establishes nations out of love and judges them with righteousness. Its polaris is the vision of a human community on earth where there is peace and good will among men because their relationships are grounded in a just and equitable social order. Its models of morality and ministry are liberators of the oppressed, advocates of the poor, contestors of greed, opponents of tyrants, and builders of community structures in which opportunities and resources are justly shared.

So a theology for the wretched of the earth will correlate the question of human misery caused by injustice with the answer of prophetic perspectives, priorities, and practices.

The import of this for the theologian is that, in order to get the raw materials for theologizing, he will have to directly and deeply involve himself with the earth's wretched and their predicaments instead of isolating himself in an academic sanctuary dreaming up new mind-trips to drain off the guilt and boredom of the privileged. It means, too, that if his faith-medicine is to have sufficient healing power, he must mix it with much less of those Biblical and ecclesiastical traditions which incline people to merely "wait and watch and pray" about demonic social conditions, and much more of the prophetic tradition which spines people to take on the pharoahs and turn an unjust world upside down.

Objective: Here-And-Now Heaven

Secondly, a theology adequate to the predicament of the earth's wretched will aim primarily at *secular salvation*; it will contain beliefs which emphasize and lead to the development of material medicines for human hurts here and now.

Mass suffering persists in a world with the resources for universal sufficiency, in part, because popular religious beliefs accept, support, and give it meaning, on the one hand, and divert attention and energy to matters quite irrelevant to realistic solutions, on the other. To their detriment and damnation, the wretched of the earth have been taught to believe that their suffering in this world is normative and irremedial, even that it is within God's will and purposes, that patient endurance of injustice is a divinely expected virtue, and that, if they pacifically bear up under such "character-making trials" on earth, they will be amply compensated in a paradise beyond the grave. Salvation, many believe, is in the future, in an other-world, an ultimate spiritual reward for deferred and deprived human gratifications in their present lives.

Such beliefs function too effectively to produce docile populations who do not take their own needs seriously enough, and don't give their oppressors trouble enough since they are preoccupied with spiritual values and life in some other realm. These doctrines may make earthly sufferings momentarily more bearable, but, in the long run, they work to produce and perpetuate the conditions which make life on this earth more unbearable. In a word, these wretched people are the victims of a religious version of the con game in which the mark is told "Look up in the sky!", and while he does, his pockets are picked.

What the planet's poor need to replace these dysfunctional doctrines of "pie in the sky by and by when they die" is a theology which emphasizes "getting their pound on the ground while they're around." Such a theology will center its attention on this world as the crucial scene of salvation where restitution for injustice can and should be made, and where lives emptied and broken by wretchedness can and should experience mending and fulfillment. Eternal life will be defined in terms of an abundant quality of human existence on earth based on an adequate material standard of living which provides freedom from want, protection from disease, and opportunity to actualize personal potential. Christ's mission will be portrayed, legitimately, as the establishment of a righteous world order in which the evils of this life are controlled and conquered by people who love one another. And discipleship, if not church membership, will be measured by actions which effectively feed the hungry, clothe the naked, teach the ignorant, and bring power and pride "unto the least" of the world's population.

In a word, this re-formed theology will provide wretched people with a faith which moves them to build their heaven on earth, not a system of other-worldly fantasies which merely takes some of the heat out of their here-and-now hell.

To construct such a theology, the theologian must become "a man of the world" in at least one important way: he will have to repent the profession's incestuous preoccupation with strictly religious and ecclesiastical matters and acquaint himself with secular fields of knowledge such as economics, political science, and law. It is especially necessary for him to understand the obstacles and resources germane to the treatment of mass material misery because the hopes he inspires must be realistic and the doctrines he develops should be translatable into practical programs. Thus, the theologian must take the world as his faith-partner in this task because the needed word will not be spoken by monologuing savants but only by conversationalists who have cared enough to search for help from any one and everyone who has a syllable to contribute.

The Morality of Selfishness

Thirdly, a theology suited to the needs of the earth's wretched should provide an *ethic of situational selfishness*;

it should deliberately offer moral justification to oppressed people for actions aimed at their self-protection, self-advancement, and liberation from misery.

One of the reasons a majority of the world's population lacks Bread is because they have been indoctrinated with self-negating ethics which prescribe attitudes and behavior which are contrary to their own interests and material improvement. Popular religious teachings have exhorted these people to deny themselves, repress and displace their appetites, sacrifice for others, go a second mile when taken advantage of, and turn the other cheek when exploited. To the extent that they internalize such morality, they develop low expectations for the satisfactions of their needs in this life, accept deprivations with virtuous resignation, and suffer guilt, if not social censure, when they aggressively pursue advantages for themselves. To the extent that they practice such morality, they get "ripped off" by the "sharks" sometimes so severely that there is little left to their lives but breath and bones.

Perhaps such a self-sacrificial ethic, if universally followed, would produce "the Good Society" in which all human needs would be equitably met out of motivation of service to others. Unfortunately, rich and powerful minorities in the world, often posing as models of altruism, have been ardent exemplars of the "virtue of selfishness" and religiously devoted to "the Greed Creed." In their quest for ever greater possessions, power, and profits, they have turned the planet into a piece of polluted property and its people into pawns. They have become scandalously opulent on sacrifices easily exacted from the miserable masses, and it is these wolves of the earth who are the real beneficiaries of the sheep's morality of self-denial.

It should be clear by now that the wretched of the earth will never be redeemed by charity from the world's affluent; that is a counterfeit hope which only helps to perpetuate the problem. The "crumbs" that are freely given are hardly commensurate with the size or kind of the hungers that exist and they often serve the counter-productive functions of pacifying legitimate urges toward social reform and creating infantile dependency on slightly benevolent oppressors.

It is equally clear that the poor and powerless will never be saved by the kind of justice provided by prevalent governmental and economic systems in which "all are equal" but the rich and powerful are always treated as "more than equal." That is not justice and should be recognized by its true name: Injustice.

In such a situation where the "have-nots" cannot rely on love or justice from the "haves," it is imperative to their earthly survival and human improvement that they learn what it means to love themselves and to consider conditions in terms of a justice which puts their own frustrated needs first.

The wretched of the earth can be encouraged and supported in this endeavor by an ethic which places supreme valuation upon equitable need satisfactions for all people, and gives strong moral sanction to selfishness in situations where people are suffering deprivations and receiving less than their fair share. This ethic should admonish rich and poor alike that no one is morally justified in increasing his welfare at the expense of those who are less fortunate. And the poor, especially, should be taught that, when unjustly deprived of their necessary and rightful portion of the world's goods and services, they are morally justified, in the name of the God of righteousness and human decency, to actively seek and serve their own self-interests.

Such an ethic would brand greed as the ugliest form of sin, and put avaricious people in social disrepute. It would score profiteering off the poor as high treason against God, and inspire efforts to make it a criminal offense. Exploitative behavior could no longer be made respectable by cloaking it with specious rhetoric about "free enterprise," "the rights of capital," and "the good of the economy"; the rights of the wretched and the enterprise of their liberation would be regarded as greater goods.

Also, this ethic would demythologize poverty—scrape it of every romantic notion used to make "poor" pretty—and judge it for what it really is: a dehumanizing condition of life, rooted in injustice, which perverts and prevents the full expression of love for lack of adequate resources and opportunities. In this ethic, poverty is not a state of beatitude but of damnation. Poverty is an evil; there is nothing nice, moral, or providential about it, and there are very few who choose it. Its widespread existence in the world, not to speak of our toleration and rationalization of it, is a mark of grave immorality. And blessed are those, even theologians, who can contribute to the work of repenting this sin.

We need not have the wretched of the earth with us always, and their salvation depends, in part, on hearing and heeding those words in the great commandment which allow self-love equal to love of others. Heaven knows that throughout history their lives have been voluntarily and involuntarily sacrificed and emptied for the satisfaction of others. Let heaven bless them now, when, still unloved by others, they struggle to love themselves.

The commission to formulate such ethics for the planet's poor demands that the theologian be responsible not just for the "truth" but also for the attitudinal and behavioral "consequences" of the ideas he sets loose in the world. It is not enough merely to make religious doctrines pass the test of compatibility with ancient authoritative traditions ("truth"). It is also of the highest urgency to discern how these beliefs are functioning and what effects they are producing in individuals and societies of this age. If the previous analysis is valid, the ethic of self-sacrifice, while "true," has disastrous "consequences" for love and justice when indiscriminately practiced by powerless people, an effect which patently contradicts what the Biblical tradition, at least, desires for the oppressed.

Thus, it becomes the crux of the theologian's task to so select, translate, and formulate "true" teachings that they have a strong possibility of producing redemptive results in the peculiar circumstances of a particular time. For him to work creatively at this tricky task is to improve the chances that his efforts will actually promote, rather than undermine, the truth and values he seeks to serve, and that history will mark him, not as a henchman of pharoahs, but a liberator of slaves.

Some Good News About Power and Politics

Finally, the theology which will help to redeem the wretched of the earth must contain *a gospel of politics and power*; it must offer teachings which correct the "bad news" image of these essential human realities, and motivate the acquisition and utilization of "clout" as a necessary, legitimate, and effective means to get Bread.

Power, in this discussion, is not to be equated with coercion and violence, although it often may be used in these ways. And politics is not to be thought synonomous with the official structures and procedures of government or the compromise of moral principles, although they are both parts of the political scene. Power refers to those resources and abilities—money, information, organizational position, votes, skill, workers—which are necessary to achieve some result or end. Politics is the art or skill of gaining and expending these resources and abilities in such a way that the goal is attained. A politician is one who can get and use power to make things happen. Nothing of importance in this world can be accomplished without the exercise of power, and politics is an elementary occupation in every area of life.

The poor and oppressed people of this earth are in their desperate predicament not because there is an insufficiency of Bread in the world, but mainly because they have insufficient power and, more importantly, because they are incompetent politicians. There is little Bread because there is little "clout," and lack of political skill is an obstacle to their salvation.

Again, the conventional religious wisdom imparted to the masses is partially responsible for these conditions. Generations of socially impotent people have been inoculated with a heavy dose of negative ideas, attitudes, and images about power, politics, and politicians which has effectively immunized them against the one fever which could restore their health. It has been preached to them, and they are quick to preach it to others, that politics is dirty, politicians are devils, power is dangerous, and religion and politics should not be mixed.

These conclusions, of course, are not reached without some experiential support. More significantly, however, when such conclusions lead the masses to a cynical withdrawal from the political arenas, they create the conditions that inevitably produce the political pathologies that disgust them. "The way things are going [Watergate], I think everybody ought to stay out of politics," said one poor woman who had not voted in years. Incontestably, power can and does corrupt, and, no doubt, "absolute power corrupts absolutely." The most devastating corruptions, however, are the result of people's abdication of power and their ignorance of political arts which leave the *machtmenschen* unchecked by countervailing forces to rule as tigers over toothless pussycats.

Salvation will draw nearer to the wretched of the earth when they have "good news" preached to them about life's political realities, and, as a consequence, they begin to have some positive experiences in political affairs. Such a gospel of power and politics will discern and proclaim power as a capital part of God's good creation, subject to no greater perversions than other parts such as religion or sex, and political action as an imperative way to do his will—at least equal to prayer and worship. It will declare the acquisition of power by the poor as a key to their liberation from oppression and misery, and the democratization of power as the necessary means for a peaceful world and the prevention of the perversion of power.

This gospel may portray Jesus as the mighty Christ of God whose mission was a power struggle with the evil forces of ignorance, disease, injustice, legalism, and death, all of which are especially destructive to the welfare of the weak, and whose signal victories over these demonic principalities gave a monumental impetus to a reign of righteousness in which the needs of the last are met first, and honor given to those who are willing and able to provide Bread and promote justice for the world's dispossessed.

This gospel should recover Moses as a major model of ministry; not just Moses the Lawgiver with the tablets on Sinai, but, especially, Moses the Liberator with the "big stick" in Egypt.

In this gospel, the church will be called to become what it could not become in the first century, but which it cannot avoid being in the modern age: an organization with enormous "clout" in the forms of money, members, knowledge, credibility, contacts, stocks, and property, which can and should be used to change social systems which grind the face of the poor in the dust and to help these downtrodden people get up on their feet. To this end, the church should be urged to educate its members in political skills so their use of power and their political involvements may be fruitful. At the same time, it can serve God and work for the world's salvation with unique distinction by becoming the teacher of political skills to the wretched of the earth. There could be no more helpful act of love!

In short, there can be no salvation without power and its skillful management in the interests of righteousness. This seems to have been God's intention. Ironically, the "children of darkness" have always recognized this piece of common sense and acted on it with a vengeance to the damnation of the weak and the blind. Perhaps the time is fulfilled and a new age is dawning when the oppressed and the "children of light" will become "wise as serpents and gentle as doves" in getting and using power so that the world's hunger and thirst for justice and love can be satisfied.

In seeking to develop such positive theological perspectives on power and politics, the theologian will probably make two discoveries which will profoundly affect his professional labors and identity. First, he will realize that, in order to speak a significant word about God and his business in the world, it is as important to scrutinize the mundane affairs of men in the present for clues to his will in order to focus attention on the flabbergasting acts of redemption in the past often identified as the "mighty acts of God." Prophets such as Amos and Jeremiah were aware of this. In doing their theology, they kept their ears close to the ground of their societies to serve better as seismographs to chart and report the current movements of God well before they erupted in cataclysmic happenings that even the blind could see. Furthermore, these men kept their ears finely tuned, to the power relations and socio-economic behavior of their times because they sensed that these were areas of crucial concern to their God of righteousness, and, if he were apt to speak to men, it would probably be about such affairs.

Thus, the modern theologian who takes seriously the poor's need for a theology of politics and who follows the methods of the prophets may find that he is not merely speaking about God, but is actually hearing God speak!

Secondly, this labor will probably lead the theologian to a corrected understanding of the role he has to play in the modern drama of salvation. Theologians may share the myopia of other intellectuals who believe that ideas are the main determinants of history, that well-phrased words make the world go around, and that they are God's vanguards because they think and speak and write about religious subjects.

In the advancing movement toward righteousness, however, actions count for more than words and ideas, one word fleshed out in a deed is far heavier than a dissertation about actions, and God's leading lances are the men and women who organize significant political actions to deliver the oppressed.

Nevertheless, the theologian as a carpenter of ideas and a mason of words does have a significant job to do in the economy of redemption. It is his humble task to discern where the Spirit of God is activating a captive people toward liberation, to join them in their struggle, to interpret their cause to the

public, and to fashion them a religious faith which will motivate, support, and justify the kind of actions which will
get them their fair share of the promised land.

This is essentially a rearguard function in the war on
wretchedness, but it is a necessary function which deserves
to be done with excellence. Thus the theologian who develops
a professional identity as a rearguard apologist for the
wretched of the earth should humbly plan on being among
the last and the least to enter the kingdom of God. But, at
least, he will make it, and that is a very exceptional achieve-
ment for a theologian.

PART III
The "How": Defining and Implementing the Church's Role

The Church's Role in Community Economic Development

SHIRLEY E. GREENE

First Principles

Nothing happens by itself.
Everybody's business is nobody's business.

It is not good enough to agree that the church ought to be supportive of poor people's self-help efforts at Community Economic Development (CED). Unless the responsibility to "do something about it" is clearly and specifically assigned somewhere and accepted by somebody, nothing will happen.

The first step is to pinpoint responsibility for initiation of the program, for coordination, and for follow-through. The assignment may be to some presently existing committee, commission, task force, or work group, or a new unit may be set up for the purpose. The important thing is that the assignment be clear and that the unit which accepts the assignment be held accountable for its performance.

For convenience, throughout this paper we refer to the responsible group in the church or judicatory as The Committee. We do not imply that The Committee is to do all the work of the church in CED and let everybody else off the hook. Quite the contrary! A few paragraphs back we used three carefuly chosen words to define the work of The Committee: "initiation," "coordination" and "follow-through." Within the scope implied in those three functional words, it is The Committee's responsibility to involve a maximum number of the constituency in the action. To spell out the implications of this paragraph is the task of the remainder of this chapter.

End Goals

Having established certain "first principles," let us leap to the other end of the spectrum and take a quick look at what we are seeking to accomplish. Then we will try to fill in the intervening steps.

What do people who are trying to help themselves through economic development projects seek from the churches? Their answers to that question are invariably the same:

We need money.

This refers to the start-up capital which any new business requires but which is not readily available to low income people's projects. Money may be in the form of grants, loans, investments, a line of credit, or loan guarantees. It is needed for feasibility studies, research and development, physical facilities, equipment, initial materials inventory, first pay rolls, and the like. In short, all the kinds of costs which are incurred before sales can take place and income begins to carry the financial load.

We need technical assistance.

Most self-help groups are composed of people of limited education and background, limited technical skills and limited experience in organization, decision making, and management of businesses. They need technical assistance of various sorts.

We need training.

This need is closely linked to the need for technical assistance. What they are really saying is that they are willing to accept initial assistance from outsiders who bring skills which they lack; but in the long run they want to learn these skills so that they can be self-sustaining and self-directed. That is the spirit and purpose of the whole self-help movement, hence the emphasis on training.

We need a supportive climate of opinion.

Self-help groups are often composed of racial and

ethnic minorities who have known a long history of oppression and discrimination. Frequently they find their efforts misunderstood, scorned, and even opposed by the established community. They seek friends who will take the trouble to know them and to understand them. They seek advocates who will support and interpret the meaning and spirit of their effort favorably to counteract skepticism and hostility in the general community.

This is the people's agenda: Money, technical assistance, training, and advocacy. Somehow the people's agenda must become the church's agenda. There may be considerable distance, however, between readiness on the part of a small group of concerned persons in a local church or judicatory and a full and generous response on the part of the church or judicatory. We now turn to an exploration of the steps which must be taken to bridge that distance.

Finding and Grasping the Handles

Rather than "ABC's" for church involvement in CED, we are proposing four "A's" for involvement: Awareness, Acquaintance, Advocacy, Assistance.

Awareness

People are not going to do something about a situation that they don't know about or respond to a need that they do not understand. There are several kinds and levels of awareness needed by The Committee itself as well as by the churches. First, we all need a greater awareness of the hard facts about poverty itself. An amazing number of people in the U.S. have little or no comprehension of the extent and depth of poverty which exists in our nation and in their own communities.

A first step for The Committee should be to discover the basic facts about poverty in the community or area as a means of heightening its own awareness and as a basis for expanding

awareness in the churches. This kind of information can be
dug out of census reports and other statistical studies, sup-
plemented by interviews with welfare officials, case workers,
community action agency people, employment service personnel, and the like.

Next, we must become aware of all that is going on in our
territory in terms of CED. Where are self-help groups already
at work? Where are others who are talking about economic
development projects and striving to get started? Where are
the pockets of poverty which need a self-help effort but
have not yet found the leadership, the initiative, or the
courage to get started?

Here again The Committee needs to confer with community action leaders, leaders in the minority and poverty
communities, staff of local development districts, and the
like. Again and again we have found local church leadership
completely oblivious to vigorous poor people's self-help efforts
going on right in their immediate community. Tragically the
church and the poor too often live in totally separate worlds
even though occupying adjacent physical space in a community or county.

A new theological awareness is also an essential ingredient.
The Committee needs to re-examine in some depth its own
Biblical and theological presuppositions about Christian responsibility for the poor and about the human goals of
Christian mission. This is not the place to develop the subject, but there is a growing literature regarding Christian
concern for justice, liberation and human development.

The Committee should early equip itself with a good solid
theological rationale for what it is doing, both as a defense
against the criticism that this is not properly "the work of
the church" and, more importantly, as the foundation for a
massive educational program throughout the churches for
expanding theological awareness and commitment by the
churches to CED.

Another aspect of awareness for The Committee involves
discovery of other groups, organizations, and agencies in the

community or area who are interested in and willing to work cooperatively with the churches in support of CED. It makes no sense for the church to try to go it alone if there are allies available. Duplication of effort, working at cross purposes, and wasting resources are among the dangers which may be avoided if all groups sharing a concern for CED can find each other and pool their efforts.

Acquaintance

Acquaintance takes us beyond awareness, beyond the realm of statistics and organizational programs to the level of personal relationship and interaction. In most communities, sad to say, a considerable gulf exists between the typical church constituency and the poor. Not only is there lack of contact; there are apt to be barriers of suspicion and hostility. The typical middle class church member is too prone to lump all poor people together with such epithets as "lazy," "shiftless," "improvident," "dirty," "stupid," and the like. The poor, on the other hand, tend to think of the middle class, including those who happen to belong to the churches, as "high brow," "stuffed shirts," "exploiters," "money grabbers," "rip-off artists," and so on.

The best solvent for these harsh mutual judgments is acquaintance. Church people must be prepared to move out personally and physically into the low income communities, the ghettoes and the barrios, and to meet people in the flesh. They must take the initiative to come to know these victims of poverty as fellow human beings. They must be prepared to do a lot of listening.

All this will take time because traditional fears and suspicions are deep-seated and will not yield quickly. There are no shortcuts. Only as genuine bonds of mutual respect and trust are formed can people from the church really become meaningful supporters of CED in low-income communities.

The Committee should assume responsibility for setting up occasions for mutual visitations between members of the church and members of the self-help group. Representatives of the self-help project can be invited to regular or special meetings at the church to describe their project and to become acquainted with church members. Tours can be arranged for church people to visit the project. Working committees can be set up to deal with specific aspects of church support for the project. By working side by side on such committees, real personal respect and trust can be expanded.

At the judicatory level, The Committee must establish acquaintance and rapport between themselves and the leaders of CED organizations and projects throughout the area. Then The Committee can arrange for contacts between church leaders and CED project leaders on a localized basis in communities where projects are situated. Conferences, consultations, and workshops where church leaders and CED project leaders are brought together for a day can be helpful. Follow-through will depend largely on local initiative, but the judicatory committee can continue to stimulate acquaintance and action in local situations.

Advocacy

The advocacy needs of CED projects are varied. Some have to do with their need for financial and technical resources. The project may be trying to sell shares for initial capital. Or the group may be in need of a line of credit at the local bank or a local supply house. Or they may be filing an application for funding with a governmental agency, a foundation, or a national denominational body.

A good word or a supporting letter from a local church leader or a judicatorial executive may make the difference between acceptance and rejection. In many cases, national funding sources require some sort of sponsorship or endorsement from a local or judicatorial body. The Committee can play that role or arrange for supportive sponsorship.

Another form of advocacy relates to the previously mentioned problem of local climate of opinion, and a beautiful illustration comes to mind. A black farmers cooperative in a rural southern community was encountéring serious hostility and harrassment from the local white community. At a one-day seminar on Economic Development as Christian Mission, a local pastor and one of his laymen were exposed to this project in a new way. Awareness and acquaintance were stimulated. The pastor prepared and circulated a simple mimeographed folder describing the work of the co-op and suggesting ways in which members of his congregation could be helpful. The laymen, who happened to own the local radio station, broadcast a series of three ten-minute comments on the co-op and its work. The result, seen through the eyes of the co-op leaders, was a major turnaround in attitudes towards their efforts. So simple! So inexpensive! Yet so crucial to the future of a people's effort at self-help.

Assistance

Finally we are back to the place where we started. The first plea of self-help groups is for assistance: financial and technical. It may seem that we are proposing a long and roundabout way of responding to that plea. Would that there were a shorter, quicker, more direct way! We are still looking for such ways, but the experience of several years suggests that awareness and acquaintance are indispensable pre-requisites for genuine and sustained support.

One note of caution: Don't put off too long the issue of direct and specific assistance. A church group can become so involved in study of the poverty problem, so involved in setting up plans and committees, so involved in just "getting acquainted," that actual participation and support may be indefinitely postponed. Moreover, there is nothing like investing some real time and some real dollars in a project to stimulate interest, acquaintance, and advocacy.

When we start talking about money, the almost automatic reply of a local church group is: "We have so little money and so many demands." Of course! Nevertheless, people do give money to churches and to church-sponsored causes. And churches give money to projects in which they believe. The question is: Do you believe in the importance of human, community, and economic development among the poor, the deprived, and the oppressed enough to channel some portion of your resources into community-based, self-help economic development? Will your church—your judicatory—respond? Let's look at two illustrations of direct response.

The first is a local church, a fairly large but not particularly wealthy church. They had just finished paying off a heavy mortgage on their building. The pastor and some lay leaders were fearful that stewardship would fall off because the pressure was off. They agreed to look for a mission project to stimulate continued stewardship. They hit upon a project in Appalachia.

Over a period of months the church raised the funds to purchase a step-van and equip it with a fine assortment of hand and power tools until it became a veritable traveling workshop. The women of the church raised money by all the means known to church women. The men did the actual work of installing work benches, power outlets, etc. At last the workshop on wheels, a $12,000 investment, was ready. It was dedicated and donated to the ecumenical agency which in turn allocated it to a builders' cooperative deep in the heart of the Appalachian mountains. Here a group of men were at work repairing and improving the homes of low income people. The step-van greatly increased the efficiency and viability of this self-help operation.

The second illustration comes from the judicatorial level. A district in the United Methodist Church in a northern state recently accepted a goal of $20,000 to be raised over four years for assistance to a comprehensive community-based economic development project among black people in a southern state. The project includes a feeder pig cooperative, a credit union, and the beginnings of a rural industrial park. The director of the project recently spent a week in the supporting district meeting with the people in several churches. There will also be visits from time to time by people from the churches to the project. These are simple illustrations of the fact that dollars can be found through regular budget channels or by special efforts when awareness and acquaintance touch the conscience and concern of the churches.

Assistance can take forms other than dollars. We have mentioned the need of CED groups for technical assistance. The Committee should develop a personnel inventory of people able and willing to contribute technical expertise to self-help groups. Look for retired business men, skilled professionals, and other non-retired persons who are willing to donate blocks of time. Among skills commonly needed are bookkeeping and accounting, marketing analysis and organization, legal advice, managerial skills, organization of work, and materials flow. Then, of course, there are needs for a great range of production skills in agriculture and manufacturing, depending on the nature of the particular project.

One illustration: A churchman from the West Coast who has made a small fortune in the food processing industry has voluntarily made several trips at his own expense to the Southeast to advise a cooperative organization which is trying to break into food processing.

Another form of assistance, not much developed as yet, but with considerable potential, is in the area of marketing the products of handcraft cooperatives. Some of these co-ops are developing beauptiful, distinctive, and high-quality handcrafts. Catalogues are now available from several of the co-ops and from some associations of co-ops. Church groups can sponsor the sale of such products either as Christmas gifts or for the personal use and enjoyment of the purchasers. Such a sales campaign might start within the church constituency and expand into the community. In some cases a local church group might take responsibility for establishing a local sales outlet for the products of a handcraft cooperative.

A Few Words of Caution

Community Economic Development is not easy. There are no shortcuts and no quick payoffs. Many self-help groups have discovered this to their dismay. Church groups motivated to support the CED efforts of the poor should understand it from the beginning.

We are talking about establishing community-based and community-controlled businesses designed to raise the income of people who have had little or no experience with the world of business. The remarkable fact is not that some of these attempts fail, but that so many of them appear to be succeeding. These comments are not intended to discourage The Committee or church groups, but to warn them against certain pitfalls. To name a few:

1. *Don't rush out and start a new CED venture without serious study of feasibility and a firm commitment to follow through.*

    In fact, little emphasis has been placed in this chapter on initiation of CED projects by the churches. Our advice to The Committee is that it first explore possibilities of relating supportively to already existing efforts. If no such possibility exists in the area, initiative by a church group may be legitimate, but it must a) avoid imposing a project from the outside on low income people; b) arrange for careful feasibility studies, and c) commit itself to stay with the project through what may turn out to be a lengthy developmental period.

2. *Don't expect instant success.*

    Experience has demonstrated that, even where most factors are favorable, the typical CED project does well to break even and begin to show profit within three to five years. Many will take longer. To stay with it may call for more persistence than church groups are accustomed to practicing. Unless there is that kind of long-range commitment, however, it is questionable whether the church should get into the game in the first place.

3. *Don't create false expectations.*

    The poor have had their fill of idle and hollow

promises from many sources. They are already suspicious of the intentions of middle class people and groups. Let us not build up their hopes once more with easy promises which we have neither the capability nor the determination to fulfill.

4. *Don't try to run the show.*

When we see a CED project making what we regard as wrong or unwise decisions, it is a great temptation to move in aggressively and try to tell the operators how to run their business. Such action will be totally counter-productive. Even if our advice is sound, it will be wrong if it is forced on the people. We can offer suggestions, but they must make the decisions. And we must respect and abide by their decisions. Otherwise it is our project; not theirs. And it will not lead to human fulfillment, no matter how successful it may be as an economic project.

Conclusion

This chapter has tried to offer some practical suggestions for the guidance of church groups in a relatively new and little-explored field of mission. It is based on the conviction that community-based, self-help forms of economic development among low income people can be an important aspect of the struggle against poverty, a potent form of human development, and a basic ingredient of genuine human community. For all these reasons it is a legitimate form of Christian mission—indeed, a mandate of Christian mission.

We began with a couple of truisms: "Nothing happens by itself" and "Everybody's business is nobody's business." Let us conclude with another: *No handbook ever administers itself.*

This manual of suggestions for implementing the church's role in CED will have no value unless it is put to work by a responsible group (which we have called "The Committee"). Moreover, The Committee will discover that the suggestions given here must be applied with imagination, must be adapted to local conditions and situations, must be used selectively, and must be ignored where they miss the mark and tailored to fit where they seem to be relevant. In short, make this chapter a guidebook, not a blueprint.

Where the Resources Are
for Rural Development

NORMAN E. DEWIRE

Although our focus is on rural *economic* development, the framework needs broadening. When asked to read from the Scriptures, Jesus turned to the place in Isaiah where it says:

The Spirit of the Lord is upon me,
He has anointed me to preach the Good News to the poor,
He has sent me to proclaim liberty to the captives,
And recovery of sight to the blind,
To set free the oppressed,
To announce the year when the Lord will save His people.

Thus the development of persons is more than economic well-being. It involves economic, spiritual, cultural, political, and human justice/dignity. In short, development is our current way of talking about the affirmation of human values.

This is the mission of the church of Jesus Christ in our day, as it was in his time and in the ages between. The ministry of Jesus was to the whole person, but with a special concern for the poor, oppressed, and suffering. Within this context, then, I want to talk about the resources available for rural development within the United States.

I. Assumptions

It is always helpful to know the bias of the author, so let me put forward four of mine:

A. The church has a Biblical imperative to express concern, through action, for the full range of human needs: personal, small group, and societal. Unless we are clear about our motivation as Christians, then what we do will be indistin-

95

guishable from other persons who do "good works." But, worse than that, we will lose sight of why we express concern, and we will tend to treat only surface problems.

B. The church has the resources to work in rural development. But how often resources are thought of only in terms of money! We have resources of time, talent, job positions of lay persons, community prestige, good will, influence, and property, as well as money. We know that development will occur when there is money available, but almost as important is the need for technical assistance, training, and a supportive climate of influence and good will.

C. The church's mission happens essentially in local communities, or it does not happen at all. We have just come through a period of church mission history when new ministries were done from the national or judicatory level in a community, but often without the involvement of the clergy and laity from that community. This tragic pattern of non-involvement is now reversed: mission occurs at the community level! This does not mean that the other levels of church organization do not have their purpose. The "middle judicatories," national agencies, national church convention, and world church organizations each have a mission responsibility to address the issues and human needs within their circles of influence.

D. You, the reader, must decide what will happen in your community for rural development. Things happen only when someone decides that they will happen. The 1970s sorely need some examples of how persons can live together, with dignity, in communities where there is caring concern. Rural development in your community will happen only if you decide to make it happen, and then act. Otherwise, these words are empty ideas in your community of need.

II. Discovery

There are some things that we need to discover very early in the process of rural development. The key words used by journalists are helpful to us here.

First, WHO are the poor? I remember a time when, in a very small community, I was asked to address two congregations about the mission opportunities of the church. Before going to that community, I looked at the census data about substandard housing, low family income, broken marriages, age distribution, occupations, educational levels, number of families on welfare, ethnic and racial backgrounds, farms, and changes in population. It became evident that there were large number of persons in that very community who needed a ministry, and this became the context of my speech on mission. In a discussion period, some denied that there were poor persons in their area. But, finally a person spoke up who was a case worker. She knew those persons that I had described, and because she knew them she was motivated to work with them. But the majority of the congregation chose to believe that there were no persons of need in their area, so the church did nothing as a group of persons. We need to know who the poor are.

Second, WHAT are the existing services? You need to discover how the community provides services to persons in need. You can find out a lot by talking with the county welfare worker, probate judge, police chief, truant officer, visiting nurse, OEO (or its successor) staff, school nurse, and mental health worker. Once you have recognized that there are poor persons in your community, you need to know the existing services for them.

Third, WHERE are the gaps between need and service? You will discover, all too quickly, what needs are not being met if you contrast the list of needs with the services being offered. If you make a personal visit with some community workers, like those mentioned above, they will tell you about the many needs they see which cannot be met through their services.

Fourth, HOW do you work? It is not possible for one person, or even one group, to be effective in rural development. You need to discover what other persons and groups are interested in working in coalition. There is so much to be done that you need colleagues who will work in coalition. To work in coalition means that we do not have to blur out differences in perspective and in methods of action. We do need to find a way to make these differences productive of a deeper practical wisdom than any of us individually can bring to the task of development. We must discover how to form a coalition of concerned persons to work together. For this author, ecumenism means working in coalition with each other.

III. Local Community

Here are some of the resources that are available in your community:

- —influence of the lay members with business, industry, government
- —in-kind technical assistance
- —climate of support and encouragement
- —local church budgets
- —local church bank deposits in new ventures
- —skills of the laity in marketing, publicity, proposal design, evaluation, office work, accounting, etc.
- —active work as a member of the local OEO agency's board
- —use of the church building and property
- —good will that can be offered
- —the fact that everyone in your community is a citizen, and thus a brother and sister with others
- —funds requested by the local church from the judicatory or national church agency to assist in community development projects

IV. Church Structures

Beyond the local community, there are three levels of church structure that have resources of skill, personnel, and funds. These three levels are the middle judicatory, national agencies, and world bodies. A judicatory is the ecumenical term used to describe the one or two church structures between local and national. This includes such entities as: district, presbytery, conference, diocese, synod, association, area, and jurisdiction. Let us look at some of the resources that are available at each level of church structure.

First, a list of some resources which the *judicatory* can offer:

—influence with county, state, and federal government for the use of their resources in development, using local development districts as a channel
—in-kind technical assistance that large numbers of lay persons can offer to groups in the communities
—benevolence or missions budget
—special fund appeals (as is often done for church building funds)
—church dollars used as leverage with government, corporations, foundations, and individuals
—deposit of funds in new ventures
—the linking of rural development with the wider resources of the metropolitan centers
—gift or loan of abandoned or under-used property and buildings
—climate of support
—requesting the use of national church funds to assist in community development projects

Second, there are a number of resources at the *national* level of the church. Each national *missions or program agency* has funds that can be used in local community development. However, as should be obvious by now, these funds are used at the request of the judicatory. The key word in obtaining national church funds is *partnership*. National agencies are not expected to develop programs in your community, but do stand ready to assist you in the development of such programs. National boards can help with ideas, examples of how things have been tried in other places, technical assistance, monitoring, and some limited funds when requested through the denominational system.

At least fifteen denominations have created special *"crisis funds."* Many of these were a result of the manifesto presented by James Forman to the National Black Economic Development Conference in Detroit, Michigan, on April 26, 1969. Some national church conventions created new self-development, or race and religion, or racial justice funds. Others expanded the use of relief funds to include domestic development. Each of these funds has developed guidelines and procedures as separate agencies from the national missions or program agency. These funds are available for local community development when the project meets their guidelines. In several denominations, part of the fund is kept at the middle judicatory, and is also available for local community development.

Several of the national missions or program agencies have made *loans* available for local community development projects. These loans are sometimes at lower rates of interest than those of local banks. Many local community development projects have difficulty securing loans in the local community; if the influence of church lay members cannot cut through some local stumbling blocks for a loan, then applications should be made for some of these national church loan funds. Related to this area is the good track record of national agencies making *deposits* in new banks which are started by racial minority persons. This is one more resource capability of the national agencies.

Third, there are some very limited resources available from *world* confessional or ecumenical *agencies.* Some world confessional groups will make grants, through their national denominational affiliate, for local community development projects. The World Council of Churches has some limited funds in four programmes—Development, Combating Racism, International Affairs, and World Service. However, since the United States is comparatively affluent, it is difficult and often unreasonable for U.S.-based projects to receive World Council assistance or to be placed on the project list.

V. Private Sector

Just as concerned persons need to work in coalition with others, so we need to look for other partners in providing resources for rural community development. We must remember that resources are more than just dollars. Various levels of govenment have numerous resources of technical assistance, guidelines, staff, and dollars. Even the smallest town now has revenue sharing funds. As long as OEO remains, there is a local community agency, with a board of citizens, who decides where OEO funds are used. You can influence these decisions, even though you are not actually part of the group that makes them.

State and federal governments constantly develop new programs and make appropriations to be used in fulfilling those programs. There are people at each state university who catalogue these programs, and they often can be helpful to concerned persons in a community who are looking for state or federal dollars. The Lutheran Resources Commission, Washington, D.C., makes a full-time monitoring of federal programs (and other private sources) and helps persons in local communities know about the programs to which they can apply.

But the real money is not to be found through government sources. The government, like the national church agencies, is interested in short-term grants in order to help a good idea get started. The funds needed to really make the difference, over the long term, must be found elsewhere.

In 1971, $21.15 billion was contributed in the United States by individuals, foundations, and corporations. Of this, 71.4% came from individuals, 14.2% from bequests, 9.7% from foundations, and 4.7% from corporations. This means that $15.10 billion (the 71.4%) came from individuals who were interested in a given program, cause, idea, or issue. That is where the real money is!

When you realize that there are at least 25,000 foundations in the United States, the $2.05 billion (9.7% of total) contributed by them is just a small amount of the total contributed. We need to know that all of the paper work, visits, and 12-18 months of waiting involved in working with foundations will only produce a relatively small amount of money. The government permits corporations to give away a small percentage of their income, but reports show that 99.9% of corporations give away far, far less than what is permitted.

Fund raising from the private sector is a very simple thing, if you will follow four basic steps. First, you need a good idea put together in a proposal package. Second, you need to do hard and full research on potential sources of support. Third, you need to develop a plan for getting to those sources, which includes visits and conversations (accompanied by someone with influence) before any proposal is actually sent.

And, fourth, you must follow through. 95% of the money comes from 5% of the people. They are the people who live in or near your community, and who are interested in its genuine improvement. Your project in rural community development might be just the idea for which they are looking!

It is possible for the church resources to be used as leverage for securing additional private sector funding. If you have decided to do something about rural development in your area, and your church (at whichever level) is supporting the project, then use this support (time, technical assistance, dollars, buildings, materials) as leverage with the private sector. It is rarely possible to raise private funds for church ministries; but it is possible to work in partnership with individuals, foundations, and corporations in funding a community-based project.

VI. Proposal Outline

The national missions and program agencies that work together through the Joint Strategy and Action Committee (JSAC) have developed an outline of basic items needed in any adequate proposal that is seeking national church funds. Each denomination may require, at whatever level of the church, some additional and special information. But, in general, this outline will serve the purpose of putting your idea into a proposal form.

I. Identification facts—name of project, full address, area to be served, date of the proposal, whether the project is being planned or when was it organized, and the date you expect funding to begin

II. Brief summary—three or four sentences summarizing long range goals and the expected length (time) of the project·

III. Project contact person's name, address, zip, and telephone

IV. Funding sources to whom the proposal is being submitted

V. Proposal planners and endorsers

   a. Local church, denominational, ecumenical units, technical specialists, and/or community agencies which were involved

   b. Representatives of the people the project will serve. How have they expressed the need for this project?

   c. The judicatories which have voted to request national church funding for this project. What commitments of their own funds have they made?

VI. Description of the situation

VII. Specific goals AND methods of evaluation for the project

VIII. Organization structure for the project

IX. Description of the action plan to be used

X. Budget

   a. An itemized list of anticipated income, by sources, for the first and second years

   b. Proposed expenditure budget for first and second years

   c. How much aid from national church agencies
   is being requested? For how long? What are the
   projected sources of income when national
   church aid is reduced and then finally stopped?

If you are going to seek private sector funding, then usually
you need to include this additional information: self-study
of the organization, case statement, corporation papers, by-
laws, annual report, long-range plan for development, organization chart, most recent financial statement prepared
by a C.P.A., and budget. It is hard to obtain private sector
funds for projects that are just starting. However, church
resources of technical assistance, volunteer time, and dollars
are available to start projects.

VII. Conclusion

There is, motivating us to action, the basic Christian goal
of the fulfillment of human beings in every community. This
includes many aspects of human life. Church folks are called
by God to engage in those small and large projects which
nurture human development. We are called upon to examine,
as Christians, the community in which we live in order to
focus on the changes that are needed.

We all stand in the need of development. Those who live
comfortably need development, just as the poor need development. While in one case it is more goods which are
needed, in the other it is more humanity. We all need each
other in the Christian quest for community.

Notes

PROFILE OF RURAL POVERTY IN THE SOUTH

1. James G. Maddox, *The Advancing South* (New York: Twentieth Century Fund, 1967), p. 5.
2. Statistics are from "State and Local Taxes in the South, 1973," a study done for the Southern Regional Council by Eva Galambos.

THE COOPERATIVE MOVEMENT AMONG THE SOUTHERN RURAL POOR

1. Albert J. McKnight, "Rural Blacks and the Cooperatives," *The American Ecclesiastical Review*, vol. CLX (Washington, D.C.: Catholic University of America Press, 1969), p. 185.
2. James Pierce, *The Condition of Farm Workers and Small Farmers* (Washington, D.C.: National Sharecroppers Fund, 1972), p. 1.
3. Mary J. McGrath, *Guidelines for Cooperatives in Developing Economies* (The University of Wisconsin, Madison, Wisconsin: International Cooperative Training Center, 1969), pp. vi-vii (paraphrased).
4. Rita M. Kelly, *The Cooperative Approach in Rural Development: A National Strategy and Program Design* (Cambridge, Massachusetts: Center for Community Economic Development, 1972), p. 1.
5. Ben Poage, *Structures for Cooperative Development* (Knoxville, Tennessee: Commission on Religion in Appalachia, 1972), p. 11.
6. *Ibid.*, p. 11.
7. William L. Hamilton, *Study of Rural Cooperatives* (Cambridge, Massachusetts: Abt Associates, Inc., 1973), p. 4 (summary).
8. Economic Research Service, USDA, *The Economic and Social Conditions of Rural America in the 1970's* (Washington, D.C.: Government Printing Office, 1971), p. 33.
9. Ray Williams and Lloyd Biser, *Analysis of Emerging Cooperatives, 1965-70* (Washington, D.C.: Farmer Cooperative Service, USDA, 1972), pp. 16-17.
10. Hamilton, p. 5.
11. McKnight, pp. 181-183.
12. Hamilton, p. 15.
13. Ray Marshall and Lamond Godwin, *Cooperatives and Rural Poverty in the South* (Baltimore: The Johns Hopkins Press, 1971), p. 21.
14. Neil Tudiver, *When Aid Doesn't Help: Obstacles to Community Economic Development in Central Appalachia* (Knoxville, Tennessee: Commission on Religion in Appalachia, 1972), p. 13.
15. In the ten co-ops expressing this goal, 48% of the members reported increased participation in the community since joining the co-op. See Hamilton, p. 6.
16. *Ibid.*, p. 16.

105

17. Tudiver, pp. 33, 34.

18. McKnight, p. 187.

19. See, for example, Ray Marshall, "The Finnish Cooperative Movement," *Land Economics* (August, 1958); and Maxwell I. Klaymen, *The Moshav in Israel* (New York: Praeger, 1970).

20. Marshall and Godwin, p. 29.

21. *Ibid.,* p. 44 (Table 2).

22. Ben Poage, "A New Heart for Central Appalachia" (Cambridge, Massachusetts: *Community Economic Development,* Center for Community Economic Development Newsletter, March, 1973), p. 4.

23. Such as the Federation of Appalachian Craft Groups (FACG), a marketing technical assistance and training organization of 43 groups, representing more than 2,000 low income craftsmen. Although fully organized, with strong assistance by CORA, the FACG never received promised OEO and ARC funds. It may also be noted, from the preceding chart, that six Appalachian co-ops, with 420 members, belonged to the Federation of Southern Co-ops in 1969.

24. The largest OEO-funded Appalachian cooperatives of the 1960's were the Southwest Virginia Growers Co-op in Nickelsville, Virginia, the Cumberland Farmers Products Corporation in Monticello, Kentucky (both vegetable marketing co-ops), the Blue Ridge Hearthside Crafts in Sugar Grove, North Carolina, and the Mountain Artisans of Charleston, West Virginia (both handcraft co-ops).

25. *Ways to Improve Effectiveness of Rural Business Loan Programs; Farmers Home Administration, Department of Agriculture* (Washington, D.C.: U.S. General Accounting Office, B-114873, May, 1973).

26. Primarily under the able leadership of David Angevine and Job Savage, FCS staff people like Dick Seymour, Francis Yager, and Ray Williams were able to greatly assist LIC development in Appalachia.

27. See Brady Deaton, *"Community Development Corporations—A Development Alternative for Rural America," Journal of Growth and Change* (University of Kentucky Press), Winter, 1975.

28. For example, Jobstart, London, Kentucky, and South East Alabama Self-Help Association (SEASHA), Tuskegee, Alabama.

29. Poage, *Structures for Cooperative Development,* pp. 7-9.

30. See *Community Development Corporations—A Strategy for Depressed Urban and Rural Areas* (New York: The Ford Foundation, 1973).

31. See *The Local Economic Development Corporation: Legal and Financial Guidelines* (Washington, D.C.: U.S. Department of Commerce, 1971).

32. Poage, *Structures for Cooperative Development,* pp. 3; 19-23.

33. By 1973, OEO Title VII Special Impact Program funds had financed one Appalachian CDC and six in the Deep South. Total federal dollars to these seven organizations in 1972 amounted to slightly more than two million dollars.

34. Current legislation to achieve this transfer was entitled The Minority Business Assistance Act of 1973 (Washington, D.C.: *Monitor,* Center for Community Change, August, 1973).

35. Stewart Perry, Center for Community Economic Newsletter (Cambridge, Massachusetts: Center for Community Economic Development, February, 1973), pp. 2-4 (abstracted).

36. As of June 11, 1973, with a total capitalization of $2,628,000. However, only three (with a capitalization of $700,000) were clearly loaning to rural projects.

37. At the time of writing, the Human/Economic Appalachia Development Corporation in Berea, Kentucky, had become the Appalachian contract agent for the Southern Cooperative Development Fund and its MESBIC, the SCDF Investment Corporation.

38. See various publications on revenue sharing distributed by Movement for Economic Justice, Washington, D.C.

39. Stephen E. Bossi, "Rural Development 1973," *Catholic Rural Life,* vol. XXII (Des Moines, Iowa: National Catholic Rural Life Conference, September, 1973), p. 8.

40. *EDA to Continue, But Other Economic Development Programs in Jeopardy* (Washington, D.C.: *Monitor,* Center for Community Change, August, 1973), p. 4.

41. See Koder Collison, *Possible Use of Section 302 to Encourage Entrepreneurship in Appalachia* (Washington, D.C.: Appalachian Regional Commission, 1973).

42. Al Ulmer, *Cooperatives and Poor People in the South* (Atlanta, Georgia: Southern Regional Council, March, 1969), pp. 26-27.

43. *Ibid.,* p. 27.

44. Marshall and Godwin, p. 95.

45. Hamilton, p. 30.

46. Mike Smathers, *Appalachia: Notes of a Native Son on Turning 31* (Clintwood, Virginia: Mountain Life and Work, Council of the Southern Mountains, February, 1973), p. 19.

THEOLOGY FOR THE WRETCHED OF THE EARTH

1. Colin Morris, *Include Me Out!* (London: Epworth Press, 1968).

Contributors

NORMAN E. DEWIRE is Executive Director of the Joint Strategy and Action Committee

GEORGE H. ESSER, JR., is Executive Director of the Southern Regional Council

SHIRLEY E. GREENE, formerly Field Secretary, Office of Town and Country Ministries, United Methodist Board of Global Ministries is now Program Secretary, Division of World Service, United Church Board of World Ministries

BENNETT D. POAGE is Executive Director of the Human/Economic Appalachian Development Corporation

DONALD W. SHRIVER, JR., is President of Union Theological Seminary in New York City. At the time of writing he was Professor of Ethics and Society at the Candler School of Theology of Emory University

HAROLD M. WAREHIME is Associate Professor of Christianity and Society at the Louisville Presbyterian Theological Seminary

THE EDITOR: JAMES A. COGSWELL is Director of the Task Force on World Hunger of the Presbyterian Church in the U.S.